Palgrave CIBFR Studies in Islamic Finance

Series Editors
Nafis Alam
University of Nottingham Malaysia Campus
Selangor, Malaysia

Syed Aun R. Rizvi
Lahore University of Management Sciences
Islamabad, Pakistan

The Centre for Islamic Business and Finance Research (CIBFR) is a global center of excellence for developing Islamic business and finance as a scientific academic discipline and for promoting Islamic financial products, monetary and fiscal policies, and business and trade practices. Based at The University of Nottingham campus in Malaysia, CIBFR looks at the multi-dimensional aspects of Islamic business, cutting across the major themes of Islamic economics, Islamic finance and the Halal market. True to the pioneering nature of the research CIBFR undertakes, the Palgrave CIBFR Series in Islamic Finance offers empirical enquiries into key issues and challenges in modern Islamic finance. It explores issues in such varied fields as Islamic accounting, Takaful (Islamic insurance), Islamic financial services marketing, and ethical and socially responsible investing.

More information about this series at
http://www.springer.com/series/15190

Shaista Arshad

Stock Markets in Islamic Countries

An Inquiry into Volatility, Efficiency and Integration

palgrave
macmillan

Shaista Arshad
University of Nottingham Malaysia Campus
Semenyih, Malaysia

Palgrave CIBFR Studies in Islamic Finance
ISBN 978-3-319-47802-9 ISBN 978-3-319-47803-6 (eBook)
DOI 10.1007/978-3-319-47803-6

Library of Congress Control Number: 2016957405

Cover illustration: Pattern adapted from an Indian cotton print produced in the 19th century

Printed on acid-free paper

This Palgrave Macmillan imprint is published by Springer Nature
The registered company is Springer International Publishing AG
The registered company address is: Gewerbestrasse 11, 6330 Cham, Switzerland

To my parents.
Thank you for everything.

Contents

List of Figures

List of Tables

CHAPTER 1

Introduction

Abstract Economists have long being interested in researching the role of financial development in the economic growth of countries. Many believe the stock market to be a barometer for economic performance, as it allocates the capital needed for consistent growth of the economy. Following the recent global crisis, attention on emerging and developing markets have increased tremendously, questioning whether these countries' market are apt in withstanding influxes of capital without crashing. The Organization of Islamic Cooperation (OIC), despite its global presence and potential, has often been criticized about its stock markets, which are marred by underdevelopment and illiquidity. This forms the main crux of this book and is explored in detail in this chapter.

Keywords Stock market · OIC · Underdevelopment · Illiquidity

The stock market plays a prominent role in the economic development of a country. It not only encourages savings and investments but also enhances corporate governance and social responsibility. A stock market, despite its relative riskiness as a mode of investment, provides great opportunities for local and global diversification through effective and efficient asset allocation. Without a stock market, economic progress and productive efficiency would remain underutilized. The stock market provides a platform for companies to raise long-term capital and for

S. Arshad, *Stock Markets in Islamic Countries*, Palgrave CIBFR Studies in Islamic Finance, DOI 10.1007/978-3-319-47803-6_1

investors a medium to invest their surplus funds. Better savings mobilization would increase the savings rate, which in turn will prompt investments and let the economy prosper.

Economists have long being interested in researching the role of financial development to economic growth of countries. Many believe the stock market to a barometer for economic performance, as it allocates the capital needed for the consistent growth of the economy. The stock market is often viewed as a leading indicator of the economy. Meanwhile, some analyst view stock markets as 'casinos', providing little impact on economic growth.

The ability of financial markets to predict correctly economic behaviour has been debated vastly over the years. Using data collected for the USA by the National Bureau of Economic Research, Siegel (1991) found that nearly always there is a decline in stock returns index, before, or right after, the beginning of a recession. Interestingly, 38 out of the 41 recessions (1802–1990) were preceded or companied by declines of 8 % in stock return index.

With much significance placed on the stock market in terms of its contribution to economic growth, it is interesting to analyse its relationship with the country's business cycle. The business cycle is commonly recognized as periodic fluctuations of aggregate economic activity. The pattern of business cycles differs from industrialized countries to those of developing countries. Business cycles in developing countries are generally shorter and more volatile than those of developed countries. Furthermore, the output fluctuations in developing countries are positively correlated with economic activity in the main industrialized countries, signifying market correlation between developed and developing countries.

The benefits of stock market inclusion in predicting business cycles outweigh its shortcomings, as it is reasonable to assume that when financial markets develop so does the economy of a country. Tobin (1964), in his seminary paper, presented his theory of financial intermediaries, in which he showed how financial policies affect aggregate demand. Schewrt (1989) has empirically established that stock prices correlate with future economic activity on the basis that economic growth forms the source of corporate profits paid out to stockholders. Hence, in theory, when the economic growth is affected, the demand and supply for equities is affected.

This forms the crux of this book whereby the objective is to examine the relationship between business cycles and stock market performance of

Islamic countries. This is done in a determination to contribute to a dearth in the empirical literature on Islamic countries. Relatively little research has been done on Islamic countries despite the fact that they comprise some of the richest countries with the largest oil and gas reserves. According to the Pew Research Center, Muslims form 23.2 % of the total world population, and are the fastest growing religious group in the world. Of this, only 20 % are residing in the Middle East–North Africa (MENA) region, and 62 % of Muslims are spread across the Asia-Pacific region.

Furthermore, Muslim majority nations are paving their way towards greater development. In terms of economic eminence, countries such as Indonesia, Saudi Arabia, Turkey and Iran are amongst some of the fastest growing economies in 2015, according to the Statistical, Economic and Social Research and Training Centre for Islamic Countries.

When discussing Islamic countries, the Organization of Islamic Cooperation (OIC) comes to the forefront as countries in the OIC are Muslim or Muslim majority. The OIC, according to its charter, aims to preserve Islamic social and economic values. In the spirit of promoting economic growth amongst member countries, the organization aims to establish an Islamic Common market to 'strengthen intra-Islamic economic and trade cooperation in order to achieve economic integration' (Organization of Islamic Cooperation 2014). As a regional bloc, the OIC plays a very significant role for Muslim countries worldwide. It provides a platform for unity and economic development of Muslims worldwide.

The OIC countries showed an increase in gross domestic product (GDP) from US$ 13 trillion in 2010 to US$ 16.2 trillion in 2014. Similarly, the average GDP per capita reached US$ 9,884 in 2014 from US$ 8461 in 2010. The OIC boasts of an annual growth rate of 6.2 % in real GDP during 2005–2007, which fell to 2.1 % in 2009 owing to the financial crisis; however, it remained positive during the crisis. Furthermore, the average real GDP growth rate of OIC countries combined remained above the world and developed countries' average. Similarly, trade among the OIC countries increased to US$ 556 billion in 2008, although dropping to US$ 421 billion in line with the global financial crisis.

Following the global crisis, OIC received 10 % of the world foreign direct investment (FDI) inflows. The FDI inflows reached US$ 132.3 billion in 2014. Within the OIC, the major recipients of FDIs in 2012 were Indonesia, Turkey, Saudi Arabia, Malayisa, UAE and Nigeria. Together these countries account for 61 % of the FDI flows to the OIC.

The increase in FDI in OIC member countries places pressure on their stock exchanges, which begs the question of whether the markets are able to withstand the influxes of capital. Currently, OIC countries' stock markets are marked with underdevelopment and inefficiency. Only 33 member countries have an active stock exchange. From this, some are newly established while others do not allow foreign participation. Many of the stock exchanges in the OIC face low levels of liquidity, which in turn increases the volatility of the stock market; this is reflected in the low number of domestic listed companies, weak market capitalization and value traded. The plight of the OIC stock exchanges is further exacerbated by inefficient and inadequate regulatory framework, lack of an effective information channel, high information cost and lack of product differentiation.

Therefore, what is observed is that, on one hand, the OIC has the potential to outperform other regional blocs, with several members being characterized as rapidly emerging markets and 21 member countries possessing total assets valuing US$ 3.3 trillion. Meanwhile, the less-developed countries are often plagued with inefficient resource allocation despite having a developing financial system. The economy often struggles to find the funds necessary to respond to increases in demand for output, consequently hampering the underlying economies. The underdevelopment and inefficiency of its stock market holds OIC from performing proficiently. As noted above, an efficient stock market plays a pivotal role in the growth of the country by allowing easy access to funds for companies to expand their business, in turn developing the economy overall.

The relationship between business cycles and stock markets will be analysed through three commanding platforms: volatility, efficiency and integration. Looking at the volatility, efficiency and integration of a stock market as an efficient market ensures that all parties are privy to the same information and risks, allowing optimal resource allocation, which in turn increases economic growth. However, the extent of efficiency in a market is often characterized by its volatility, whereby the higher the volatility, the more unpredictable it would seem to market players and hence reduce its efficiency. Additionally, national and international events often pave way for high volatility in stock markets, indicating that integration plays a significant role in the volatility of the stock markets.

Furthermore, as a country becomes more attractive to foreign investors for diversification, stock markets are able to increase their liquidity and informational transparency allowing for higher degrees of efficiency and integration. On a macroeconomic level, it is argued that financial integration tends to improve financial infrastructure, as it leads to improved allocation of resources, enhancing both consumption and income risk sharing and reduces volatility of consumption growth. Additionally, as linkages increase, it can also lead to adoption of international accounting standards and a closer monitoring of the market, allowing markets to be more transparent. Hence, in an environment where increasing linkages improve the domestic market, problems of asymmetric information are curtailed and efficiency is maximized.

Hence, what we can see here is that the volatility, efficiency and integration of a stock market are related and are vital in analysing the performance of the stock market. Understanding the relations of efficiency, integration and volatility of a market with the different phases of the economy will allow investors to make more informed investment decisions.

The first part of our investigation analyses how short-term traders and long-term investors are affected by stock market volatility during different business cycle phases in the OIC. Using a multistep process, comprising of bandpass filters to obtain the business cycles, wavelet to decompose the stock returns and Exponential General Autoregressive Conditional Hetrosckedascity (EGARCH) to obtain the volatility, the volatility of OIC member countries' stock markets during expansionary and recessionary stages of the business cycle is assessed.

The second part empirically examines the efficiency of the stock markets to gauge the financial market development of Islamic countries. A stock market is said to be efficient if the current price reflects all the information included in the past price. Therefore, as stock prices incorporate all vital information, the returns should be based on a random pattern. If stock prices were predictable, there would be distortions in the pricing of capital and risk, thus inhibiting economic development.

This is accomplished in a three-way analysis. First, the 12 sample OIC countries are ranked according to their efficiency for the entire sample period, that is, from 1998 to 2015. Second, the efficiencies of the sample country will be ranked throughout six major regimes, covering three crisis periods (i.e. the Asian Financial crisis; the 2000–2002 period marred by accounting scandals, like Enron, WorldCom and the dotcom crisis; and the 2008–2010 global crisis). Third, each country is studied individually to analyse its efficiency during each business cycle turns.

Employing a current trending method of econophysics; multifractal detrended fluctuation analysis (MFDFA), the efficiency rankings are obtained.

The third part undertakes the analysis of market integration of OIC countries with the global benchmark. The central aim is to examine comparatively the extent of underdevelopment of stock markets in the OIC vis-à-vis more developed stock markets. Furthermore, the level of integration with the world for both groups of countries is measured. Following in the footsteps of the International Capital Asset Pricing Model (CAPM), the market integration of 10 OIC countries and 3 developed countries is measured. This analysis covers an overall market integration with world averages, then each individual market focusing on the integration level for each turn of the business cycle and lastly, each market's integration with three major world regions, that is, the USA, Asia-Pacific and the European Union is assessed using MGARCH.

Following the introduction in Chapter 1, the remainder of the book is divided into six chapters. Chapter 2 provides some background on business cycles, while Chapter 3 discusses the economic situation of the OIC and its stock markets. After this, the focus is on analysing each of the three platforms, whereby volatility is discussed in Chapter 4, efficiency is analysed in Chapter 5 and the market integration is presented in Chapter 6. Lastly, Chapter 7 concludes the book, along with some policy implications.

References

Organization of Islamic Cooperation. (2014). *About OIC*. http://www.oic-oci.org/oicv3/page/?p_id=52&p_ref=26&lan=en. Accessed 16 June 2016.

Schewrt, G. W. (1989). Why does stock market volatility change over time?. *The Journal of Finance*, *Xliv*(5), 1115–1153.

Siegel, J. J. (1991). The behaviour of stock returns around N.B.E.R. turning points: An overview (Working Paper No. 5-91). *Weiss Centre Working Papers*. Research Document. http://finance.wharton.upenn.edu/weiss/. Accessed 24 June 2016

Statistical, Economic and Social Research and Training Centre for Islamic Countries. (2015). *OIC Economic Outlook*. OIC. Resource document. http://www.sesric.org/files/article/517.pdf. Accessed 12 June 2016.

Tobin, J. (1964). Economic growth as an objective of government policy. *American Economic Review: Papers and Proceedings*, *54*, 1–20.

CHAPTER 2

Background on Business Cycles

Abstract The chapter provides some background on business cycles. When discussing business cycles, it becomes necessary to define clearly recessions and expansions. The National Bureau of Economic Research (NBER) defines recession as a period between a peak and a trough, and expansion as a period between trough and a peak. Furthermore, the different types of cycles and theories associated with business cycles are discussed. A key theory that is relevant in this book is the Real Business Cycle (RBC) theory. According to the theory, changes in technology in the business sector cause the booms and bust of a business cycle.

Keywords Business cycle · Real business cycle · Expansion · Recession

2.1 Description of Business Cycles

In one of the early works of the National Bureau of Economic Research (NBER), Burns and Mitchell (1947) (page 3) developed an encompassing definition of business cycles as follows:

> Business cycles are a type of fluctuation found in the aggregate economic activity of nations that organize their work mainly in business enterprises: a cycle consists of expansions occurring at about the same time in many economic activities, followed by similarly general recessions, contractions, and revivals which merge into the expansion phase of the next cycle; this

S. Arshad, *Stock Markets in Islamic Countries*, Palgrave CIBFR Studies in Islamic Finance, DOI 10.1007/978-3-319-47803-6_2

> sequence of changes is recurrent but not periodic; in duration business cycles vary from more than one year to ten or twelve years; they are not divisible into shorter cycles of similar character with amplitudes approximating their own.

Cassel (1922, p. 550) described business cycles as following: a 'period of boom is one of special increase in the production of fixed capital; a period of decline or a depression is one in which this production falls below the point it had previously reached'. He explain that the variations between periods of boom and bust are fundamentally changes in the production of fixed capital, but does not have any direct connection with the rest of the production. He believed that changes in cost and value of capital goods are the main driving forces of the economy's cyclical formation.

Hodrick and Prescott (1980) and Baxter and King (1999) define the business cycle as the stationary component that is remnant after the output is passed through an ideal bandpass filter. Their definition relies mainly on the frequency components of the data. An alternative to this definition relies on the unobserved component view of the output, whereby the output is the sum of an unobserved trend and cycle.

When discussing business cycles, it becomes necessary to define clearly recessions and expansions. A more generally recognized definition is provided by the NBER, which refers to recession as a period of decline in economic activity shown through two consecutive quarters of decline in a country's real gross domestic product (GDP).

Furthermore, the NBER defines recession as a period between a peak and a trough, and expansion as a period between trough and a peak. A recession is categorized as a significant decline in economic activity spread across the economy, lasting more than a few months, normally visible in real GDP, real income, employment, industrial production and wholesale–retail sales. Similarly, they classify an expansion as a substantial rise in economic activity typically lasting several years.

Here forth, the definitions provided by the NBER are used, whereby a recession typically last more than 6 months. Furthermore, this book will rely on Industrial Production Index as a representation of the economy. Shorter business booms or busts are not included as the focus is on the study of fundamentals, the impact of which comes from longer periods of recessions and expansions. Taking shorter periods of contractions and expansions becomes unnecessary to this analysis owing to its lack of impact on a country's fundamentals.

2.2 The Different Types of Cycles

This section briefly distinguishes between the different types of cycles used to explicate economic fluctuations. First, we have business cycles as discussed above. Second, the Kondratieff cycle is used to explain long cycles. Kondratieff (1935) identified economic long waves in Western countries of approximately 50–60 years. In his theory, each cycle consists of three phases: expansion, stagnation and recession. Later economists divided these three phases or waves into four seasons, whereby spring represented improvement, summer showed acceleration and prosperity, fall was indicative of a plateau and winter was decline and depression.

Entrepreneurs bringing about social shifts of expansion and growth led the first season. Summer represented escalating prosperity that changes the general attitude towards work leading to inefficiency and complacency. The plateau period represented by fall comes next as social attitude shifts towards stability and normalcy. It is at this period that unemployment rises. Lastly, winter is the stage of severe depression, where the economy suffers significantly. However, modern economists do not accept this long wave theory, with much of the criticism pointing towards undecided start and end periods of the waves.

Third, the technology cycle, as discussed by the Real Business Cycle (RBC) theory, suggests that there is a high positive correlation between labour productivity and employments.

2.3 Theories of Business Cycles

One of the earliest theories linked fluctuations to that of harvest, and since harvest is depended on nature, it was considered a biological cycle. However, this theory was not without its critics and it did not last long at the turn of the twenty-first century when the contribution of agriculture had fallen significantly. The best-known sector cycle in economics is the agricultural commodity cycle, which followed the cobweb pattern. Kaldor (1938) explained that regular fluctuations occur in agricultural production because (1) the following period's production is dependent on current or past prices, and (2) the current prices are also determined by current production.

With the introduction of the Industrial Revolution at the end of the eighteenth century, technology and technological revolutions have spurred many economists to conclude that technological innovation had brought about a wave of change in the economy without end but rather with pauses in between. Hence, these rhythmic changes in technological innovations could be responsible for corresponding movements in the economy. The most popular and well-established theory in this aspect is the RBC theory, which is discussed in detail below.

Another popular theory lies in the imbalance between output and sales in an expanding economy. This has led economics to believe that business cycles are caused by either overproduction or underconsumption. The Keynesians are strong proponents of this theory. Similarly, other theories hold that changes in supply of savings and investments that come along with it cause waves in the economy. Lastly, monetary theorist are of the opinion that changes in money supply cause economic fluctuations; in such an increase, the total quantity of money could cause an increase in economic activity. One such theory, the Austrian Business Cycle (ABC) theory is explored in detail below.

Below the RBC theory is discussed in detail owing to its relevance to this book and other theories are mentioned briefly.

2.3.1 Real Business Cycle Theory

A key theory that is relevant to this book is the RBC theory. According to the standard RBC approach, the competitive equilibrium of the market economy achieves resource allocation that maximizes the representative household's expected utility given the constraints on resources. Although the RBC approach has often been criticized for its abstraction from firm and household heterogeneity.

According to the theory, changes in technology in the business sector are what cause the booms and bust of a business cycle. It argues that macroeconomic variables are largely responsible for shifts in business cycles. The RBC theory demonstrates that changes in economic activity are compatible with competitive general equilibrium environments. Therefore, factors such as coordination failures, price stickiness, waves of optimism or pessimism or monetary or fiscal policy are not needed to explain business cycles.

Proponents of the RBC theory believe that only the forces that can change the Walrasian equilibrium can cause fluctuations in economy. The Walrasian equilibrium is described as the set of quantities and relative prices that brings together supply and demand in all markets of the economy at the same time.

On the other hand, opponents of the RBC theory argue against the viability of the RBC theory saying that there is a lack of rigorous economic testing to test the practicality of how it explains business cycles. Similarly, the theory does not account for recessions, as it would require economy-wide reduction in productivity.

It is argued further that the RBC model does not account for monetary shocks, while much evidence is available to suggest that monetary conditions stimulate business cycle fluxes. New Keynesians have considered this limitation and worked upon a better fitting theory on business cycles.

Another interesting critique on the RBC Models is its use of the Hodrick–Prescott (HP) filter to decompose series into growth and business cycle components, as it removes valuable information associated with business cycles and can cause spurious data patterns.

2.3.2 *Keynesian Theory of Business Cycles*

Keynesians commented on the classical view asserting that the demand would not be able to self-correct in an economy due to an impotence of money, that is, the failure of real GDP to respond to increases in real money supply or a decrease in real interest rates. Similarly, they argue that supply side would also not be self-correcting because of a failure to maintain equilibrium wages in the labour market.

Keynes (1936) asserts that the most important factor generating business cycles is fluctuations in efficiency of capital. Accordingly, a boom caused mainly by excessive investments is compelled by the increase in marginal efficiency of capital. Similarly, he states that economies recover regularly from recessions due to the depreciation of excess capital stock accumulated during boom. This will eventually return to normal levels within several years.

The Keynesians, like RBC theory, also attempt to predict increases in real interest rate through temporal increases in government purchases (demand side); however, they do not give much importance to the effect of real interest rate on labour supply. The proponents of the Keynesian theory of business cycles choose to focus more on the macrodynamic explanations of business cycle fluctuations.

2.3.3 Austrian Business Cycle Theory

Developed by Mises (1912), it is based mainly on conservative macroeconomic variables of savings, money supply, interest rates and investments. Fundamentally, the theory argues that because of the monetary authority's ability to expand the money supply, there would be an impact on interest rates, saving and investments, which causes business cycles.

According to Mises, the most essential determinant of business cycle is the impact of monetary expansions on interest rates. This is so because when more money is available in the economy, it becomes cheaper for investors to borrow to expand their investments, and choose to invest in long production processes thereby shifting consumption from present to future. This concept, advanced by Hayek (1935) who argued that the business cycle growth because of credit creation, is not sustainable because the fall in interest rates is not a permanent phenomenon.

The ABC theory, however has limitations, in that, it over emphasizes the impact of interest rates. Interest rates on their own may not create the effects that ABC theory asserts. Increased investments after a fall in interest rates can be a result of other economic factors. The mainstream economics ascertain that credit expansion leads to inflation, suggesting that business cycles produce inflation. The Austrian position has not integrated this economic fact in their analysis. The ABC theory does not hinge on there being any inflation during the business cycle boom. However, inflation is always a monetary fact and cannot be denied.

The ABC theory also ignores the rational expectation hypothesis. The theory fails to explain the ability of people to distinguish between an increase in personal savings and an increase in central bank holdings of government debt, which is an important and reasonable requirement of individual rationality in economic actions.

References

Baxter, M., & King, R. G. (1999). Measuring business cycles: Approximate bandpass filters for economic time series. *The Review of Economics and Statistics, 81*(4), 575–593.

Burns, A. F., & Mitchell, W. C. (1947). Measuring business cycles. *Journal of the American Statistical Association, 42*(239), 461–467.

Cassel, G. (1922). *Money and the foreign exchange after 1914*. New York: Macmillan.

Hayek, F. A. (1935). *Prices and production*. London: Routledge.

Hodrick, R. J., & Prescott, E. C. (1980). *Post-war U.S. business cycles: An empirical investigation* (Working Paper No. 451). Retrieved from Carnegie-Mellon University.http://www.kellogg.northwestern.edu/research/math/papers/451.pdf.

Kaldor, N. (1938). Professor Chamberlin on monopolistic and imperfect competition. *The Quarterly Journal of Economics, 52*(3), 513–529.

Keynes, J. M. (1936). *The general theory of employment, interest and money.* London: Macmillan.

Kondratieff, N. D. (1935). The long waves in economic life. *The Review of Economic Statistics, XVII*(6), 105–115.

Mises, L. (1912). *Theory of money and credit.* New Haven: Yale University Press.

CHAPTER 3

Overview of the Organization of Islamic Cooperation

Abstract The chapter provides a detailed description of the Organization of Islamic Cooperation (OIC) and its stock markets. As the second largest regional bloc, the OIC is home to several rapidly emerging markets and natural resources-rich countries. Despite this, out of the 57 member countries, only 33 have an active stock exchange. In these, there are significantly lower domestic companies listed as compared to other developing and emerging markets. Less liquid markets bring about an increased volatility, and an increased volatility is reflective of both shallowness and a lack of integration with global markets, indicating the main problem with OIC stock markets.

Keywords Stock market · Economic development

3.1 Introduction

As one of the largest intergovernmental organizations, second only to the United Nations, the Organization of Islamic Cooperation (OIC) boast a 57-state membership spreading over four continents. It was established in 1969 with the intention of bringing together and protecting the interest of Muslims from around the world.

From an economic perspective, the OIC consists of three different categories of countries: low-income, middle-income and high-income countries. Hassan et al. (2010) divide the member countries into 3 groups

S. Arshad, *Stock Markets in Islamic Countries*, Palgrave CIBFR Studies in Islamic Finance, DOI 10.1007/978-3-319-47803-6_3

to analyse its economic performance. First, the Least Developed Members (LDC) comprise countries classified as least developed by the United Nations, namely, Afghanistan, Bangladesh, Benin, Burkina Faso, Chad, Comoros, Djibouti, Cambia, Guinea, Guinea-Bissau, Somalia, Sudan, Togo, Uganda and Yemen.

Second, the Middle-Income countries (MDC) such as Albania, Cameroon, Cote d'Ivoire, Egypt, Guyana, Indonesia, Jordan, Kazakhstan, Kyrgyz Rep, Lebanon, Malaysia, Morocco, Pakistan, Palestine, Surinam, Syria, Tajikistan, Tunisia, Turkey and Uzbekistan. Lastly, the third subgroup consists of high-income, oil-exporting countries such as Algeria, Azerbaijan, Bahrain, Brunei, Gabon, Iran, Iraq, Kuwait, Libya, Nigeria, Oman, Qatar, Saudi Arabia, Turkmenistan and the UAE.

There are significant resources and potentials in the OIC to stimulate growth and development. According to Statistical, Economic and Social Research and Training Centre for Islamic Countries (SESRIC), the total gross domestic product (GDP) of OIC countries witnessed an increasing trend in economic activity and the GDP increased from US$ 13 trillion in 2010 to US$ 16.2 trillion in 2014. While the average GDP per capita in OIC countries increased from US$ 8,461 in 2010 to US$ 9,884 in 2014. From Fig. 3.1, we can see the growth trend from 1990 until 2014. The GDP of OIC member countries have been steadily rising since the 1990s until the 2001 September 11 attacks, which caused oil prices to soar and the rest of the world to be wary of Muslim countries. Similarly, prior to the 2008–2009 global financial crisis, the GDP was increasing significantly. However, after the crisis, growth trends have remained sluggish.

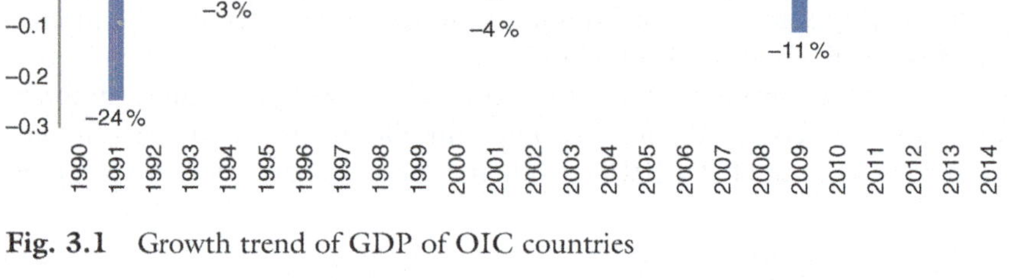

Fig. 3.1 Growth trend of GDP of OIC countries

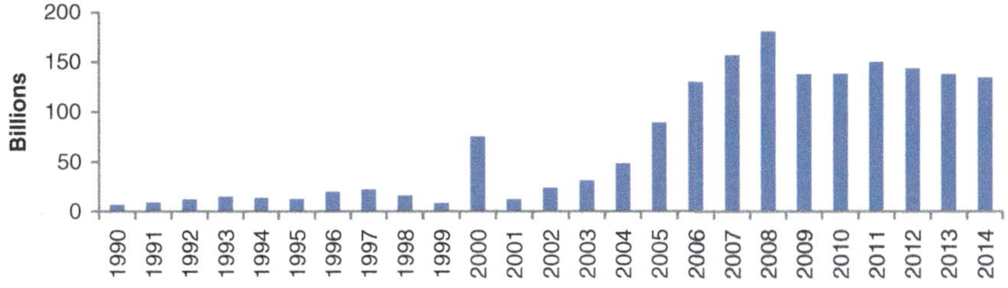

Fig. 3.2 Net Foreign direct investment flow to the OIC (in current US$)

In line with the economic slowdown worldwide, trade and investment flows were severely affected after the 2008 crisis. Figure 3.2 shows net foreign direct investments (FDIs) to the OIC reducing after the global crisis and several internal crises faced by the OIC member countries. In 2014, OIC member countries attracted US$ 132 billion in FDIs as compared to US$ 144 billion in 2011.

Despite the increase in FDI and the potential benefits that can help member countries, the firms in the OIC countries remain dormant in their pursuit of better market opportunities created by globalization, for instances taking advantage of lower cost of production. Some countries can take advantage of lower costs in fellow member countries thus improving their competitive strength.

However, with the recent global crisis, trade with global powerhouses such as USA, EU, Japan and other developed countries have significantly reduced and OIC member countries are now looking towards trade cooperation amongst themselves. The share of intra-OIC trade in 2014 reached 19.9 %. Initially, this was initiated by regional economic cooperation schemes that sometimes included non-OIC member countries. Four major subgroups were formed, namely, Arab Maghreb Union (AMU), Council of Arab Economic Unity (CAEU), the Gulf Cooperation Council (GCC) and the Economic Cooperation Organization (ECO).

3.2 Salient Features of OIC Member Countries Economy

The section will discuss some of the salient features of the OIC member countries' economy. Out of 57 countries, only 33 have an active stock exchange. Hence, this book will be focusing on these countries. However, despite the presence of a stock exchange, either many of these countries have no proper data available or the data available are not long enough for a conclusive analysis. Owing to this, several countries were excluded. The economy of countries included in this book is discussed below.

3.2.1 Malaysia

Malaysia is considered an upper-middle income economy, which is the third largest in Southeast Asia. According to the Commission on Growth and Development report by World Bank, Malaysia was one of the 13 countries to have recorded average growth of more than 7 % for 25 years or more. Malaysia has succeeded in nearly eradicating poverty, whereby the number of households living below the poverty line is less than 1 % currently (World Bank 2016b).

Following this economic boom and rapid development over the past few decades, Malaysia's GDP per capita was US$ 11,062.043 in 2014. After the Asian financial crisis of 1997–1998, Malaysia continued to post solid growth rates, averaging 5.5 % per year from 2000 to 2008. While, the global financial crisis hit Malaysia in 2009, it recovered rapidly, posting growth rates averaging 5.7 % since 2010. This is owing to strong fundamentals in the economy.

The official religion of Malaysia is Islam, where Muslims make up to 61.3 % of the total population and is declared an Islamic state. It has been a founding member of the OIC since 1969 and has held several Islamic conferences in a bid to open dialogue between Muslim countries.

3.2.2 Indonesia

Indonesia has the largest economy in Southeast Asia and is one of the emerging market economies of the world. Indonesia's economy was affected greatly by the Asian financial crisis of 1997. Its rehabilitation required monetary help from International Monetary Fund (IMF). Economic growth accelerated to 5.1 % in 2004 and reached 5.6 % in 2005. Indonesia managed to skirt the recession of 2008, helped by strong domestic demand (which makes up about two-thirds of the economy) and a government fiscal stimulus package of about 1.4 % of GDP. Indonesia is the third fastest growing economy in the Group of Twenty (G20) industrialized and developing economies after India and China (International Monetary Fund 2014).

Muslims make up 87.2 % of the total population, making it the largest democratic Muslim-dominated country in the world. However, it is a Muslim-majority country and not an Islamic state. Indonesia has maintained good bilateral relations with almost all OIC members, and recently hosted the fifth summit of the OIC.

3.2.3 Pakistan

The economy of Pakistan is the 26th largest in the world in terms of purchasing power parity (PPP) and 40th largest in terms of nominal GDP. Pakistan is characterized as a developing country, and is one of the Next Eleven countries set to become one of the largest economies in the twenty-first century. Despite an unstable economy susceptible to external and internal shocks, the Pakistani economy has proven to be resilient in the face of multiple adverse events. However, in 2008 the IMF had to bail out Pakistan to avert a balance of payment crisis. Overall, liberalization and growing stability in monetary policies have contributed to the high performance of the economy. However, Pakistan faces significant economic, governance and security issues that impede development.

As an Islamic republic, Muslims make up 96.4 % of the total population and has strong ties with OIC member countries. Pakistan has significant militarily cooperation with Saudi Arabia, Indonesia, the UAE, Brunei, Nigeria and other Middle Eastern Countries.

3.2.4 Bangladesh

The Bangladeshi economy is the 32nd largest in the world by PPP and is among the Next Eleven emerging market economies in the world. According to IMF, Bangladesh's economy is the second fastest growing major economy of 2016, with a rate of 7.1 %. Throughout last decade, Bangladesh averaged a GDP growth of 6.5 %, leading the country to becoming an export-oriented industrialization. Foreign aid has seen a gradual decline over the last few decades but economists see this as a good sign for self-reliance. There has been a dramatic growth in exports and remittance inflow, which has helped the economy to expand at a steady rate. In the past decade, the economy has grown at nearly 6 % per year (World Bank 2016a), improving human development, whereby the poverty has dropped by nearly a third since 1992.

While it is not an Islamic state, Islam is the largest religion in the country, with Muslims constituting 89.5 % of the population. Its relationship with the OIC calls for state members to show support for the Islamic University of Technology in Bangladesh. The export of Bangladeshi to the OIC reached US$ 1579.55 million in 2013.

3.2.5 *Turkey*

The IMF has defined the Turkish economy as an emerging market economy and a developed country according to the Central Intelligence Agency (World FactBook: Turkey 2012). Turkey has the world's 18th largest nominal GDP. The country is a founding member of the Organisation for Economic Co-operation and Development (OECD) (1961) and the G20 major economies in 1999. Turkey is also a part of the EU Customs Union since 1995. Muslims form the majority of the population at 97.8 %. Furthermore, the level of intra-OIC trade with Turkey was at US$ 77.8 billion in 2014.

During the recent global financial recession the Turkish economy expanded by 9.2 % in 2010, and 8.5 % in 2011. It stands out as the fastest growing economy in Europe, and one of the fastest growing economies in the world. This was owing to the Turkish government introducing various economic stimulus measures to reduce the impact of the 2008–2012 global financial crisis in 2009. Turkey is also a source of foreign direct investment in Central and Eastern Europe and the Commonwealth of Independent States (CIS), with more than US$ 1.5 billion invested.

3.2.6 *Jordan*

Jordan is a Muslim majority country constituting 95 % of the population. The IMF has classified Jordan as an emerging market. In 1999, liberal economic policies were introduced that resulted in a boom that continued through 2009. Jordan has a developed banking sector that attracts investors due to conservative bank policies that enabled the country to weather the global financial crisis of 2009. Jordan's economy has been growing at an annual rate of 7 % after King Abdullah II's accession to throne in 1999 and upto 2008. As of 2015, Jordan boasts a GDP worth of US$ 37.6 billion, ranking it 89th worldwide. The main obstacles to Jordan's economy are scarce water supplies, complete reliance on oil imports for energy and regional instability. Its trade ties with other OIC member countries reached 33 % in 2014.

3.2.7 *Egypt*

Islam is the prevailing religion in the country with Muslims comprising 94.7 % of the population. Egypt has had an unsteady economy over the past decades. Under comprehensive economic reforms initiated in 1991, Egypt had relaxed many price controls, reduced subsidies, reduced inflation, cut taxes and partially liberalized trade and investment.

In the 1990s, a series of IMF arrangements, coupled with massive external debt relief resulting from Egypt's participation in the Gulf War coalition, helped Egypt improve its macroeconomic performance. Post the global crisis of 2008, soaring food prices led to calls for the government to provide more immediate assistance to the population. Egypt faced the long-term supply- and demand-side repercussions of the global financial crisis on the national economy.

3.2.8 *Nigeria*

Nigeria is a middle-income, mixed economy and emerging market. It is ranked as the 21st largest economy in the world in terms of nominal GDP, and the 20th largest in terms of PPP, and it is the largest economy in Africa. About half the population is Muslim and Nigeria's relationship with the OIC goes towards the D-8 group, where it has significant trade links with the countries.

In 2012, Nigeria received a net inflow of US$ 85.73 billion of FDI (World Bank 2016c). The economy has enjoyed sustained economic growth for a decade, with annual real GDP increasing by around 7 % from 6.3 % in 2014.

3.2.9 *Kuwait*

Islam is the official religion in Kuwait. Kuwait is a high-income economy which is backed by the world's sixth largest oil reserves. In 2015, the Kuwaiti currency was the highest valued currency unit in the world. Kuwait has nearly 10 % of the world's oil reserves. Petroleum accounts for nearly half of GDP and 95 % of export revenues and government income. Kuwait is the Arab world's largest foreign investor, with US$ 8.4 billion in FDI outflows in 2013.

3.2.10 *The UAE*

The economy of the UAE is the second largest in the Arab world with a GDP of US$ 570 billion in 2014 (World Bank 2016d). Although the UAE has the most diversified economy in the Gulf Cooperation Council (GCC), the UAE's economy remains extremely reliant on oil. Dubai suffered from a significant economic crisis in 2007–2010 and was bailed by Abu Dhabi's oil wealth. A massive construction boom, an expanding manufacturing base and a thriving services sector are helping the UAE diversify its economy.

3.2.11 *Qatar*

Qatar is now the richest country in the world (Pasquali 2016). Oil has given Qatar a per capita GDP that ranks among the highest in the world. Oil and gas account for about 85 % of export revenues and over 50 % of GDP. Qatar has oil reserves exceeding 25 billion barrels, and its natural gas reserves are the world's third largest.

3.2.12 *Oman*

Oman's economic performance improved significantly in 1999 largely due to the mid-year upturn in oil prices. In 2000, Oman liberalized its markets helping its economic performance. In 2015, low global oil prices drove Oman's budget deficit to US$ 6.5 billion, or nearly 11 % of GDP. Oman has limited foreign assets and is issuing debt to cover its deficit.

3.3 OIC Member States Stock Markets

As mentioned earlier, only 33 out 57 states have an active stock market. The oldest stock market in the OIC countries dates back to 1933 when the Egyptian stock exchange was established. Several of the stock markets are fairly new and underdeveloped. A list of OIC countries with stock exchanges is provided in Table 3.1

The main companies listed in the OIC stock exchanges are from the following sectors: real estate, tourism, mining and metals, IT, consumer

Table 3.1 National stock exchanges of member countries

	Country	*Stock Exchanges of Member Countries*
1.	UAE	Abu Dhabi Securities Exchange
2.	Jordan	Amman Stock Exchange
3.	Bahrain	Bahrain Bourse B.S.C. (c),
4.	Azerbaijan	Baku Stock Exchange
5.	Beirut	Beirut Stock Exchange
6.	Turkey	Borsa Istanbul
7.	Algérie	Bourse d'Alger
8.	Malaysia	Bursa Malaysia Berhad
9.	Morocco	Casablanca Stock Exchange
10.	Bangladesh	Dhaka Stock Exchange
11.	Syria	Damascus Securities Exchange
12.	Cameroon	Douala Stock Exchange
13.	Egypt	Egyptian Exchange
14.	Indonesia	Indonesia Stock Exchange
15.	Iraq	Iraq Stock Exchange
16.	Pakistan	Karachi Stock Exchange
17.	Kazakhstan	Kazakhstan Stock Exchange
18.	Sudan	Khartoum Stock Exchange
19.	Kuwait	Kuwait Stock Exchange
20.	Kyrgyz Republic	Kyrgyz Stock Exchange
21.	Libya	Libyan Stock Market
22.	Maldives	Maldives Stock Exchange
23.	Mozambique	Mozambique Stock Exchange
24.	Oman	Muscat Securities Market
25.	Qatar	Qatar Stock Exchange
26.	Kingdom of Saudi Arabia	Saudi Arabian Stock Exchange
27.	Iran	Tehran Stock Exchange
28.	Albania	Tirana Stock Exchange
29.	Uzbekistan	Toshkent Republican Stock Exchange
30.	Tunisia	Tunisia Stock Exchange
31.	Uganda	Uganda Stock Exchange
32.	Nigeria	Nigerian Stock Exchange
33.	Palestine	Palestine Securities Exchange

goods, financial services and so on. Despite high development potential, the OIC stock exchanges are often characterized with low levels of liquidity, seen through a low number of listed companies, low market capitalization and low stock trading volume. Table 3.2 shows these three characteristics for some OIC member countries. The data obtained from World Bank were available for the following 17 countries only.

Table 3.2 Descriptive statistics for OIC stock markets

	Market capitalization/GDP (%)				
	1994	*1999*	*2004*	*2009*	*2014*
Bangladesh	3.0	3.0	4.8	20.4	–
Egypt, Arab Rep.	–	–	–	48.3	23.2
Indonesia		45.7	28.5	39.8	47.4
Iran, Islamic Rep.	3.9	19.2	23.2	14.8	27.4
Jordan	–	–	–	133.6	71.3
Kazakhstan		–	9.1	24.2	10.1
Kuwait	40.1	66.5	122.7	–	–
Malaysia	247.1	176.8	145.6	143.0	135.8
Morocco	–	–	–	74.2	47.9
Nigeria	16.5	8.2	18.1	19.0	11.2
Oman	16.5	26.6	38.1	46.4	46.2
Pakistan	24.9	11.1	46.5	19.0	–
Qatar	–	–	–	66.4	88.5
Saudi Arabia	–	–	–	74.3	64.1
Turkey	16.5	45.1	25.1	37.7	27.5
UAE	–	–	37.5	54.5	50.5
	Number of listed domestic companies				
	1994	*1999*	*2004*	*2009*	*2014*
Bangladesh	157	348	185	197	274
Egypt	–	1032	795	312	246
Indonesia	217	276	331	398	506
Iran	142	295	404	364	315
Jordan	95	151	192	272	236
Kazakhstan	–	18	75	70	68
Kuwait	41	76	108	–	196
Malaysia	475	749	955	952	895
Morocco	56	54	53	76	74
Nigeria	177	194	215	214	188
Oman	100	134	225	120	117
Pakistan	724	765	639	629	557
Qatar	–	–	–	44	43
Saudi Arabia	–	–	73	135	169
Turkey	176	286	253	248	226
UAE	157	348	185	197	274

Table 3.2 (continued)

	Value traded/market capitalization (%)				
	1994	*1999*	*2004*	*2009*	*2014*
Bangladesh	10.6	62.0	6.2	11.2	–
Egypt	–	–	–	81.5	37.7
Indonesia		33.0	29.9	40.0	21.5
Iran	15.4	8.1	26.4	28.7	20.0
Jordan	–	–	–	40.5	12.1
Kazakhstan	–	–	25.8	15.3	3.8
Kuwait	19.3	40.7	66.5	–	–
Malaysia	6.5	30.1	29.8	28.0	31.1
Morocco	–	–	–	–	5.8
Nigeria	1.5	3.8	10.6	13.9	8.2
Oman	14.3	11.6	20.9	26.0	15.3
Pakistan	0.5	297.2	307.7	55.2	–
Qatar	–	–	–	–	29.4
Saudi Arabia	–	–	–	105.1	117.4
Turkey	100.3	60.3	149.1	135.0	168.2
UAE	10.6	62.0	6.2	11.2	–

From the market capitalization to GDP ratio, it is observed that stock markets represent a small percentage of the GDP, particularly for Bangladesh, Egypt, Kazakhstan and Tunisia amongst others. Typically, a value greater than 100 % means that the stock market is overvalued. It is interesting to note that this occurred mainly during crisis times. For most of the countries, the value is higher during the 2009 period, resultant of the ongoing crisis at that time. Figure 3.3 shows that over the past 20 years there has been a progressive increase in the market capitalization to GDP ratio, indicating an increasing importance of stock markets in the recent years to the OIC member countries. Malaysian and Jordanian stock market appears to the most overvalued in their respective regions owing to their size and volume of trade.

Next, as seen in Table 3.2, there has been little change to the number of listed domestic companies with the exception of some countries. Elucidating this, in Fig. 3.4, Malaysia has the highest number of domestic companies listed in the Asian region while Egypt until 2002 had the highest number. In the 5 years to 2007, Egypt lost 713 companies owing to recessions, economics and political instability.

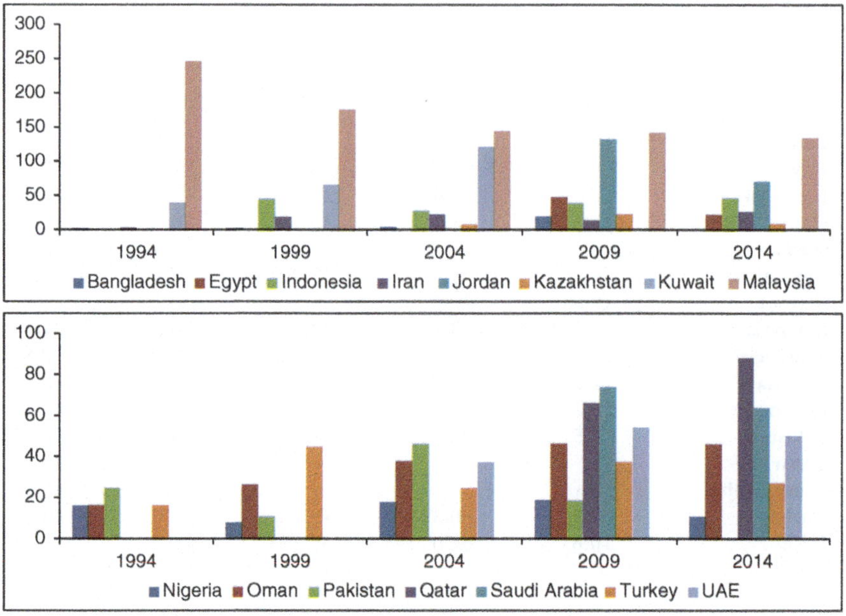

Fig. 3.3 Market capitalization/GDP for OIC member countries

Overall, the OIC has significantly lower domestic companies listed as compared to other developing and emerging markets. Yu and Hassan (2009) attribute the low liquidity in OIC stock markets to this lack of listed domestic companies. Further exacerbating the liquidity problem is the underdeveloped regulatory frameworks and macroeconomic risks assigned to these markets.

Less liquid markets bring about an increased volatility, and an increased volatility is reflective of both shallowness and a lack of integration with global markets. This reflects the inherent problem of stock markets within the OIC.

Moving on, Table 3.2 shows the value traded/market capitalization rate. This provides information on the total value of the shares during the period divided by the average market capitalization for the period. Malaysia, once again performed the highest on this proxy amongst the Asian members of OIC, whereas, Kuwait remained consistently high over the years. Turkey ranked the highest for the year 2009, as seen in Fig. 3.5.

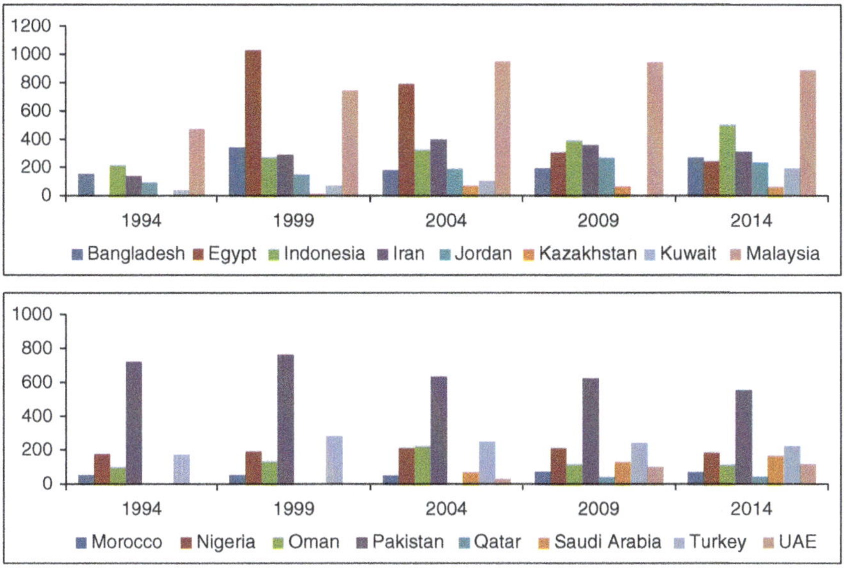

Fig. 3.4 Number of listed domestic companies for OIC member countries

From the above descriptive statistics of the OIC member stock markets it can be assessed that, with the exception of a few, markets are marked with underdevelopment, low market capitalization, low number of listed domestic companies. These issues are exacerbated with most of the markets still in their infancy stage, a lack of a prominent regulatory framework to guide them. Furthermore, some of the markets are still closed to foreign participation making them unable to develop further.

Incongruously, these issues create a wall for further economic development of the OIC countries. Given the economic prominence and attention the OIC countries are receiving from development markets for development purposes, it becomes necessary for OIC member states to optimize their stock markets. The following chapters aim to build a case for the stock markets in three vital aspects, that is, volatility, efficiency and integration. Understanding where the OIC member states stand with these aspects can help formulate policies to allow for better wealth management and efficient investments, which in turn promotes economic development.

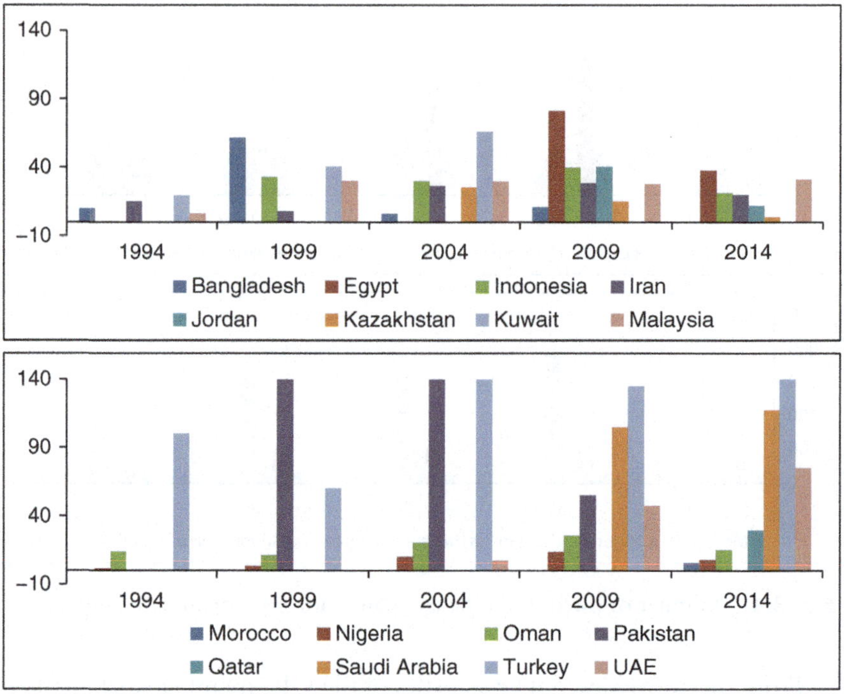

Fig. 3.5 Value traded/market capitalization for OIC member countries

References

Hassan, M. K., Sanchez, B. A. & Hussain, M. E. (2010). Economic performance of the OIC countries and the prospect of an Islamic common market. *Journal of Economic Cooperation and Development*, *31*(2), 65–121.

International Monetary Fund. (2014). *IMF Survey: Indonesia's Choice of Policy Mix Critical to Ongoing Growth*. Resource document. http://www.imf.org/external/pubs/ft/survey/so/2009/car072809b.htm. Accessed 11 June 2016.

Pasquali, V. (2016). The richest countries in the world. *Resource document. Global Finance Magazine*. https://www.gfmag.com/global-data/economic-data/richest-countries-in-the-world?page=12. Accessed 19 June 2016.

World Bank. (2016a). Resource document. *Bangladesh Overview*. http://www.worldbank.org/en/country/Bangladesh/overview. Accessed 19 June 2016.

World Bank. (2016b). Resource document. *Malaysia Overview*. http://www.worldbank.org/en/country/Malaysia/overview. Accessed 19 June 2016.

World Bank. (2016c).Resource document. *Nigeria Overview*. http://www.worldbank.org/en/country/Nigeria/overview. Accessed 19 June 2016.

World Bank. (2016d).Resource document. *UAE Overview*. http://www.worldbank.org/en/country/UAE/overview. Accessed 19 June 2016.

World FactBook: Turkey. (2012). Central intelligence agency. Resource document. https://www.cia.gov/library/publications/the-world-factbook/geos/tu.html. Accessed 11 June 2016.

Yu, J.-S., & Hassan, M. K. (2009). Rational speculative bubbles in the OIC stock markets. *IIUM Journal of Economics and Management*, *17*(1), 97–131.

CHAPTER 4

Vetting the Volatility

Abstract The Organization of Islamic Cooperation (OIC) comprises several rapidly growing industries attracting large sums of foreign direct investments. The emerging nature of the markets and the rapid influx of investments bring about the question of how the stock markets in OIC member countries react to variations in the economy. The objective of this chapter is to understand the relationship between business cycles and stock market volatility within the OIC member countries for short-term traders and long-term investors. The results showed that most of the OIC countries, being oil rich and dependent, saw its business cycle and stock markets fluctuating owing to drops and increases in world oil prices. All the countries in the sample were affected by the global crisis.

Keywords Volatility · Christiano–Fitzgerald filter · Short term · Long term · EGARCH

4.1 Introduction

A large majority of Organization of Islamic Cooperation (OIC) member countries are developing and emerging markets, which tend to experience larger and more volatile fluctuations in business cycles than their developed counterparts. They are often characterized by a severe fall in asset prices after economic recessions especially following periods of asset-priced boom.

S. Arshad, *Stock Markets in Islamic Countries*, Palgrave CIBFR Studies in Islamic Finance, DOI 10.1007/978-3-319-47803-6_4

The OIC has witnessed its fair share of economic recessions, for example, Malaysia and Indonesia, in particular, were affected significantly by the 1997 Asian financial crisis. Turkey, Pakistan, Kuwait and other countries suffered from internal crisis, bank runs, stock market crashes and political instability respectively over the past two decades. Furthermore, the degree of financial development varies substantially across the OIC in particular. Some countries, such as Malaysia, Turkey, Jordan and the Gulf Cooperation Council (GCC) countries, are advanced with well-developed financial, banking, insurance and other financial institutions. Whereas, other member countries lag behind in their financial development stage and invite more room for improvement of the institutional environment and financial sector.

This chapter will analyse the volatility of OIC member countries during different business cycle phases to understand how volatility affects short-term traders and long-term investors differently.

4.2 Why Study Volatility?

One of the main models explaining the key connection between financial markets and macroeconomic volatility is the financial market imperfection model. In their seminal paper, Greenwald and Stiglitz (1988) describe a model incorporating the impact of financial market imperfections caused by asymmetric information in the market, which could lead to breakdowns. The principal concern with information imperfections is that it restricts the ability of a firm to raise equity funds in external capital markets. Hence, this can have negative macroeconomic implications in the economy. Additionally, they were able to confirm empirically that after ruling out macroeconomic factors, financial markets accounted for certain aspects of actual business cycles.

Another widely accepted view is by Bernanke and Gertler (1995) who postulated a hypothesis known as the 'balance sheet view', which says that changes in monetary policies impact the balance sheet (net worth) of a firm and consequently the overall economy. Further, it argues that 'financial accelerator' variables such as lagged output, sales or cash flows augments these nominal and real shocks to an economy. The financial accelerator effect suggests that adverse economic conditions lead to a fall in aggregate investments, due to shifts in the credit supply curve caused by increases in asymmetric information costs.

Third, according to fundamental valuation models, stock prices depend on expectations of the future economy, hence changes in real activity leads the stock prices. However, in accordance to the wealth effect, changes in stock prices cause variations in the real economy. Hence, both theories suggest that the stock market predicts the economy. Shirai (2004) and Mun et al. (2008) are among some of the economists who argue that a larger increase in stock prices reflects economic growth in the future and large decreases in stock prices is an economic recession indicator. Correspondingly, Hamilton and Lin (1996) in their paper found that stock market downturns precede economic recession, while stock market upsurges anticipate business cycle. This allows stock market indices to constitute as a leading indicator for economic activity.

4.2.1 Relationship Between Stock Markets and Business Cycles

The relationship between financial activity and business cycle has been researched empirically with varied opinions. Earlier studies have shown stock market volatility to be countercyclical; where it was greater in recessionary periods than in expansions. Furthermore, the correlation between stock market and industrial production cycles are significantly positive. This would mean that periods of low financial volatility usually prevail during stock market and real economic boom and vice versa.

The stock market is a leading indicator of economic activity, whereby fluctuations in stock prices have a direct effect on aggregate spending. Hence, as the stock market is rising, investors are more likely to spend more resulting in an expanding economy. The same holds true when stock markets are declining, investors spend less causing a slower economic growth.

On the other hand, several scholars do not agree that stock markets can be a predictor of economic activity. They contend that stock markets have previously garnered false signals about the economy and hence cannot be trusted as an economic indicator. Barro (1989) found that stock prices predicted three recessions for the years 1963, 1967 and 1978 that did not occur.

Siegel (1991) also highlights that stock markets are prone to false alarms, especially in post-war periods in America. He stresses that there were 12 episodes since 1802 where the cumulative return index has dropped by at least 8% and yet this was not followed by a recession within 12 months. Stock market or financial development in general has often been viewed as a means of developing the economy.

However, despite some false alarms, the importance of stock markets to real economic activity is significant. An efficient financial system provides a buffer against severe output contractions. Empirical research on the development of capital markets and its impact on macroeconomic erraticism have drawn the conclusion that development of the capital market leads to lower macroeconomic volatility. Countries with more developed financial sectors experience smaller fluctuations in real per capita output, consumption and investment growth.

4.2.2 *Within the OIC*

Narrowing in on the OIC, a significant absence of stock markets are seen in most OIC member countries whereby only 33 out of 57 countries have an active stock market, where most of them are fairly new with low stock volumes. A lack of developed stock markets in most Muslim countries can be attributed to the fact that many Muslim-headed households and enterprises voluntarily exclude themselves from financial markets citing religious requirements (Mohseni-Cheraghlou 2013). With the prevalence of interest in conventional markets, many Muslims refrain from active participation.

A 2010 Gallup poll indicated that 90% of adults living in OIC member countries considered religion as a vital part of their daily lives. This would further explain why only 2.5% of adults in OIC member countries have bank accounts in any form of financial institutions.

The OIC member countries' stock markets offer significant potential portfolio diversification benefits for investors but access to most of the stocks have been limited to international investors. For instance, among all the OIC stock markets in the Middle East and North Africa (MENA) region, only Morocco and Egypt have allowed international investors unrestricted access. Meanwhile, Saudi Arabia despite having the 12th largest stock market amongst emerging markets did not allow direct investment from non-GCC nationals until recently. Similarly, in the South Asian and sub-Saharan division of OIC countries, the stock markets are relatively less developed and illiquid.

This causes a distortion in the information disseminated to international investors as compared to other emerging financial markets. The only exception in OIC comes from the East Asian markets, whereby Malaysia and Indonesia have successfully attracted substantial amounts of foreign and portfolio investments.

4.3 Methodology

The methodology consists of a three-step process to investigate the relationship between business cycle and volatility. In the first step, the business cycle is constructed using a bandpass filter to detrend the Industrial Production (IP) index. In the second step, wavelet is used to decompose the stock data into short term and long term and lastly, in the third step the volatility of stock is calculated using Exponential General Autoregressive Conditional Hetrosckedascity (EGARCH).

4.3.1 Formulating the Business Cycle

A bandpass filter is a device that passes frequencies within a certain range while rejecting frequencies that are outside the range. This analysis uses the Christiano–Fitzgerald bandpass filter to detrend the business cycle data.

This analysis uses the IP index in its derivation of the business cycle. The use of the IP index as a proxy for business cycles stems from many empirical researches supporting its significance and ability to reflect correctly the economy. The International Monetary Fund (IMF) conceptualizes the IP index as a business cycle indicator, which shows the changes in output of an industry. By definition, the IP index measures changes of industrial activities from one period to another. As this study requires high frequency data to measure the business cycle, and not all of the countries selected produced quarterly gross domestic product (GDP) data, IP is used as the proxy for GDP.

It has become progressively popular to characterize the behaviour of macroeconomic variables using a set of uncontroversial summary. Detrending or compiling facts of the business cycle gained relevance as it gives a coarse theory of the multifaceted comovements and provides benchmarks that can be used to validate numerically theoretical models. Nelson and Plosser (1982) in their protuberant paper suggested that macroeconomic time series are better characterized by stochastic trends than by linear trends, hence leading to the increasing use of filters to identify permanent and cyclical components of time series.

The Christiano and Fitzgerald (2003) filter is based on the assumption that the data generated by a random walk are nearly optimal. Hence, they do not assume the weights to be symmetrical. The Christiano–Fitzgerald filter uses the whole time series for the calculation of each filtered data point. The Christiano–Fitzgerald filter has a steep frequency response function at the boundaries of the filter band (i.e. low leakage); it is an asymmetric filter that comes together in the long run to the optimal filter. It chooses the weights for the moving average filter to minimize the mean squared error between the filtered series based on the ideal filter and the filtered series based on their approximation. Furthermore, the filter assumes a random walk process without drift.

Benefits of the Christiano–Fitzgerald filter are that it produces results that are more accurate for long-term business cycles and is better suited for times series where characteristics of the cycles at the beginning and end are of importance. A detailed explanation on the methodology of the filter can be found in Christiano and Fitzgerald (2003).

4.3.2 Decomposition of Stock Returns

Daily market index is collected and the daily return on the market index is calculated from the index value. After calculating the return series for every market index for each of the sample countries, wavelet analysis is used to separate each return series into its constituent multiresolution (multihorizon) components. To do that, Maximum Overlap Discrete Wavelet Transformation (MODWT) is applied on daily return series by sampling the return series at evenly spaced points in time. It transforms the return series from time domain into scale (interval) domain to understand the frequency at which the activity in the time series occurs. In this analysis, the daily return series is sampled at different scale crystals (j) as follows: *d*4 (16–32 days), *d*5 (32–64 days) and *d*6 (>64 days).

The non-decimated orthogonal MODWT with *symmlet 8* is used as a wavelet function to obtain a multiscale decomposition of the return series. The MODWT will be used with the advantage on the flexibility of the length of data (not requiring the integral power of two) as well as time invariant property. The wavelet family *symmlet 8* is chosen to get the least asymmetry property, which is more appropriate for financial series. Wavelet analysis contains the coefficients for the father wavelet at the maximal scale called the 'smooth' coefficients that represent the underlying smooth behaviour of the series and 'detail' coefficients that represent the scale deviations from the smooth process.

The wavelet method is beneficial over other conventional filters for many reasons. First, wavelet filtering is capable of deconstructing complex signals without significant data loss. Second, it is able to separate the minute details from larger fluctuations from a single series. Third, wavelet allows decomposing a single time series into many components, that is, it provides a multiresolution analysis for correlation. Hence, allowing the study of the correlation's dependence on a time scale. This is important because different investors have different investment horizons and wavelet analysis can be used to improve decision making in the practical situations of risk management, portfolio allocation and asset pricing.

4.3.3 *Volatility of Stocks*

The next part of the analysis consists of the evaluating the volatility of the stocks for which Exponential General Autoregressive Conditional Hetrosckedascity (EGARCH) is used. The standard GARCH model allows the conditional variance to be dependent upon its past. It has some limitations whereby it cannot account for the leverage effects, and does not allow for any direct feedback between the conditional variance and conditional mean. Owing to these reasons, since the focus is on volatilities, the practical asymmetric GARCH model EGARCH developed by Nelson (1991) is used.

This model benefits from no parameter restrictions and allows for more stable optimization of routines. Furthermore, EGARCH helps in capturing asymmetric responses in the conditional variance at a more superior level. However, even this is not without some drawbacks, the EGARCH model is not able to fit financial returns in which the market shocks have a non-normal conditional distribution. If the returns are measured at a daily frequency, market returns have skewed and leptokurtic conditional returns. This is the case for this book, where the returns for the stock indices are calculated at a daily frequency. Nevertheless, despite certain shortcomings, EGARCH is considered one of the best method available to investigate the volatility of stocks.

4.4 Data Used

Two sets of data are employed: the first set consists of the daily market index for stock markets from 11 OIC member states. The second set consists of monthly Industrial Product of each country selected to form the business cycle in each of these countries. Owing to a lack of available stock market data on OIC countries, this research contains a varying time span for different countries. This ensures optimal usage of available data and findings that are more robust. The market indices obtained are from the Morgan Stanley Composite Index (MSCI) family group rather than individual market index to maintain homogeneity in data source. As different indices have different ways of calculating indices, the MSCI is used to reduce the risk of dissimilarity in indices.

Due to the emerging nature of majority of the OIC member countries, a lack of readily available data circumscribes this research. The countries that will be used are selected, first on their latest market capitalization and second on the availability of data for that particular country. The countries pass a two-step criterion in order to be selected, first, they need to be one of the 10 highest-ranking countries by market capitalization, as this shows how well the market is doing based on the market size and secondly, it has to have a minimum of 10 years of historic data available. This is to ensure robustness of results.

Owing to the differing economic advancement of OIC member countries, a balanced time period could not be selected to avoid loss of key information, an imbalanced time period is selected decidedly based on the number of years the stock market has been active and data are available. A list of the countries selected is presented in Table 4.1.

Figure 4.1 ranks the OIC member countries with an active stock market according to their market capitalization. Market capitalization is used as an indicator owing to its economic significance as it provides information on how well the market is doing based on market size. Data on stock markets and business cycles were available for all but Iran and Morocco, which ranked 7th and 10th respectively within the OIC for market capitalization. Hence, in an effort to compensate this loss, two

Table 4.1 List of countries selected

	Country	*Coverage period*
1.	Malaysia	1990–2014
2.	Indonesia	1990–2014
3.	Saudi Arabia	1998–2014
4.	Turkey	1990–2014
5.	Qatar	1998–2014
6.	UAE	1995–2014
7.	Kuwait	1995–2014
8.	Egypt	1993–2014
9.	Nigeria	1995–2014
10.	Pakistan	1990–2014
11.	Jordan	1990–2014

Fig. 4.1 Market capitalization of OIC member countries in 2014

additional countries were included in the analysis, that is, Pakistan and Jordan. The Karachi Stock Exchange (KSE) of Pakistan is one of the largest in South Asia by means of market capitalization, hence making it a worthy stock market to explore. Similarly, the Amman Stock Exchange (ASE) of Jordan has been reporting an annual increase of 36% on average since 2000 and has been consistently performing well.

4.5 Results and Discussions

The relationship between stock market volatility and business cycle is analysed by first breaking up the business cycle into boom and busts periods. Second, the stock market volatility is divided into short term and long term. These classifications allow to see clearly, first, the changes in volatility during different business cycle periods and second, how short-term traders and long-term investors are affected in different economic conditions.

Figure 4.2 provides a clearer picture on the business cycles using the Christiano–Fitzgerald filter. As can be seen from the graphs, the business cycles are more frequent and of varying lengths. Furthermore, all of the countries showed dips in the business cycle graphs during the global crisis of 2008.

Moving on, the daily stock returns were decomposed through the Maximum Overlap Discrete Wavelet Transform (MODWT) as this provides

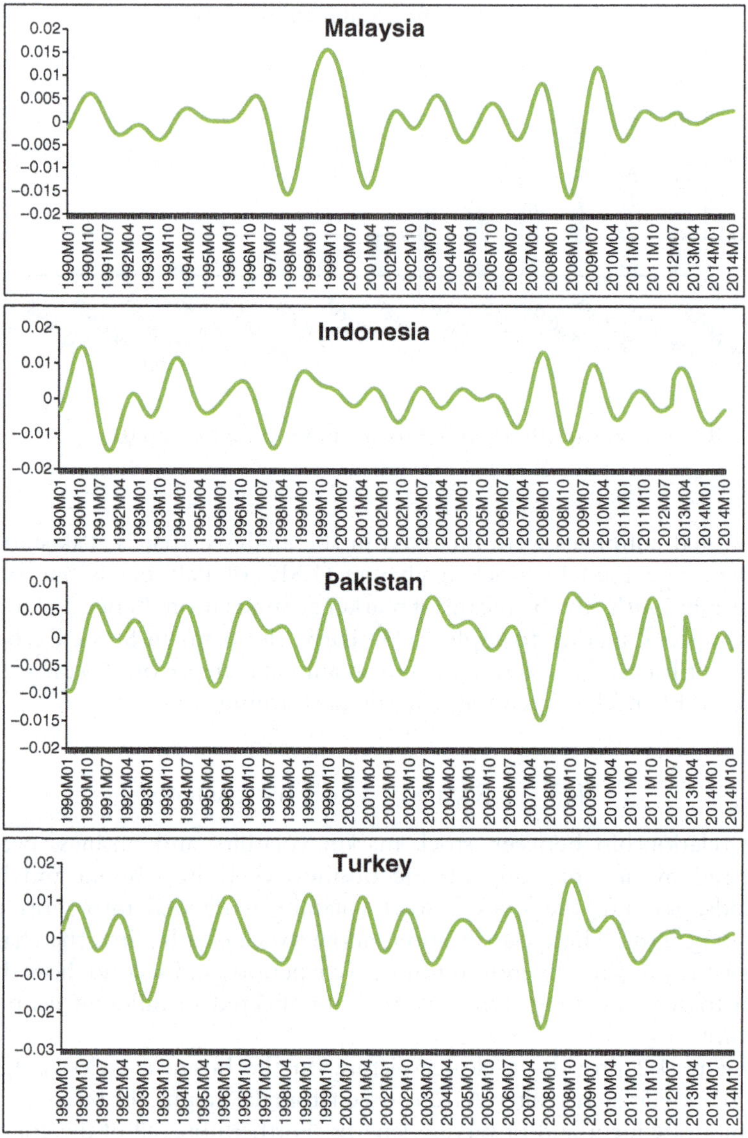

Fig. 4.2 Graphs of business cycles of sample countries

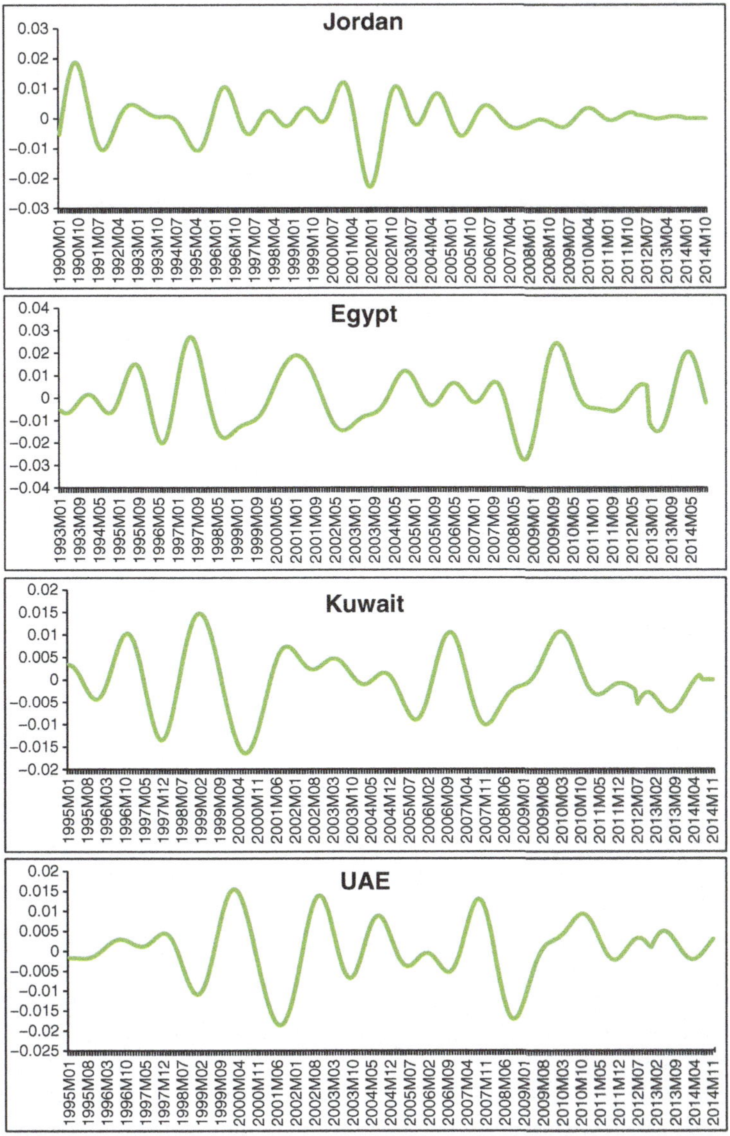

Fig. 4.2 continued

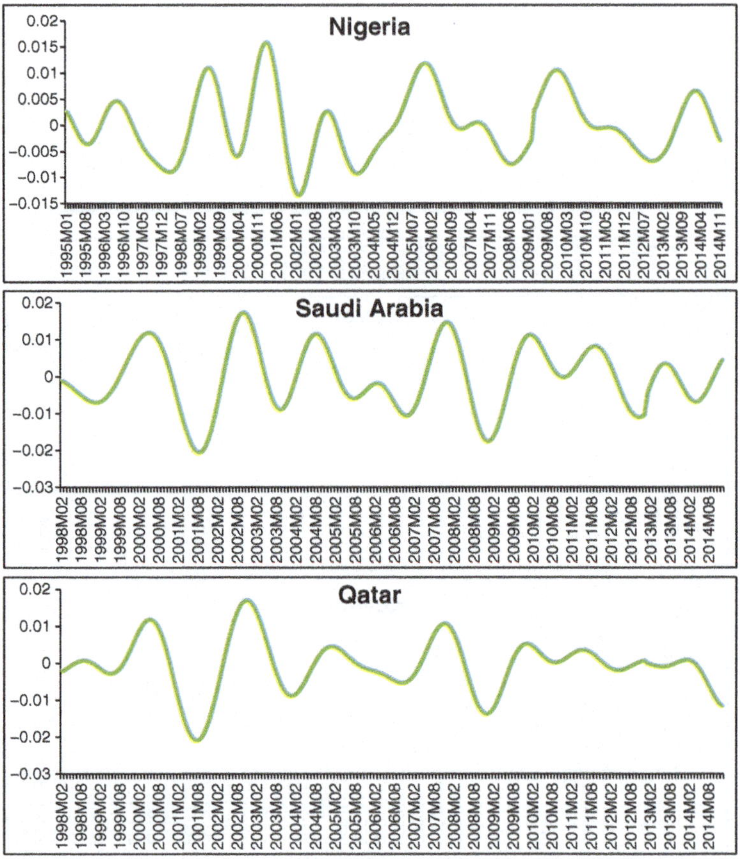

Fig. 4.2 continued

the benefit of flexibility of length of data as well as time invariant property. The wavelet family *symmlet 8* is chosen for the least asymmetry property, as it is more appropriate for financial series.

Each index return is proportioned into five time scales of detail and one time scale of approximation. The detail will contain high-frequency component (short horizon) while the approximation will contain smooth part (long horizon). The five time scales of detail from the lowest to the highest represents 2–4 days, 4–8 days, 8–16 days trading, 16–32 days and 32–64 day and an approximation scale representing over 64 days. The fifth scale and approximation scale is recomposed to become denoised stock returns.

As the objective is to analyse the behaviour of stock markets and business cycles for short and long term, the 6 scales are fused into 3 segments. First, the original series is presented, second, for the short-term investigation, the scales 2–4 days, 4–8 days are added up to represent short term, that is, up to 8 days scale. Third, 32–64 days and over 64 days are added up to become the denoised returns and this represents long-term investments. This is done to simplify the explanation of the impact of stock market volatility on investors and traders alike during different business cycle phases.

Prior to a detailed study on the countries, Table 4.2 records the mean volatility of stock returns for the sample countries. Owing to a large number of observations, the variances obtained are small and can be misleading, hence for a better understanding, first, the standard deviation of the variances is obtained and second, it is scaled to a multiple of 1000, for presentation purposes.

From Table 4.2 we see that the original series, that is, before it was decomposed into short- and long-term scales, the volatility remained on average near 24 with the highest coming from Indonesia at 114 and lowest being the UAE stock market at only 7.89. UAE also had the lowest volatility in the denoised returns, while in the short run volatility remained average at 2.4 suggesting that the market is well developed and efficient.

Table 4.2 Descriptive statistics for EGARCH on sample countries

	Mean volatility		
	Original	*Short Term*	*Denoised*
Malaysia	11.5015	2.1144	1.9347
Indonesia	113.9815	2.4241	2.5426
Pakistan	13.511	2.3743	2.6214
Turkey	25.1161	4.1271	3.7766
Jordan	9.0551	1.5191	1.4173
Egypt	13.5758	2.5306	2.4982
Kuwait	23.8368	1.5577	1.5879
Nigeria	10.9809	3.6337	1.5701
UAE	7.8870	2.3958	1.0058
Saudi	12.7625	2.1000	2.0844
Qatar	22.3470	2.2790	2.1320

In the next part of the analysis, the volatilities and its relationship with business cycles for each country individually are studied.

4.5.1 *Malaysia*

Table 4.3 portrays a variegated pattern of volatility for the Malaysian market. The Malaysian market had similar levels of volatility throughout both periods, with the exception of the Asian financial crisis of 1997, where negative IP growth rates reported, averaging at -0.95% for the crisis period. It is also when the stock market volatility was highest averaging at 30.95 for the original series and around 5.3 for both the short-run and long-term scales. Moreover, it is seen that the economic effect and stock market volatility moved in tandem. As the economy began to unravel in late 1997, the stock market volatility also spiked in the same period. This indicated that short-term traders reacted to the economic crisis.

Interestingly, for the period of expansions in March 1990–September 1991, January 1999–August 2000 and June 2009–June 2010, the volatility was higher than in the subsequent recessions. For instance, in the boom cycle of 1999 the volatility for short-term and long-term investors

Table 4.3 Business cycle and volatility for Malaysia

		IP growth	*Stock volatility*		
		Avg. Growth (%)	*Original*	*Short Term*	*Denoised*
1990M03–1991M09	Boom	0.3345	12.295	2.432	2.016
1991M10–1994M02	**Recession**	**-0.2001**	**10.319**	**2.054**	**1.878**
1994M03–1997M07	Boom	0.2020	11.311	1.935	1.656
1997M08–998M12	**Recession**	**-0.9449**	**30.95**	**5.252**	**5.526**
1999M01–2000M08	Boom	1.0477	16.705	3.012	3.095
2000M09–2002M01	**Recession**	**-0.8522**	**12.941**	**2.54**	**2.396**
2002M02–2004M06	Boom	0.2057	8.764	1.713	1.533
2004M07–2005M06	**Recession**	**-0.2666**	**6.685**	**1.323**	**0.827**
2005M07–2006M06	Boom	0.2700	5.343	1.022	0.816
2006 M7–2007M03	**Recession**	**-0.2478**	**8.140**	**1.576**	**1.721**
2007M04–2008M03	Boom	0.5197	11.985	2.318	1.664
2008M04–2009M05	**Recession**	**-1.0042**	**13.027**	**2.183**	**2.246**
2009M06–2010M06	Boom	0.7346	6.934	1.332	1.037
2010M07–2011M03	**Recession**	**-0.2615**	**2.048**	**1.192**	**1.081**
2011M04–2014M12	Boom	0.1580%	6.549	1.084	0.844

was 3.012 and 3.095 while the accompanying period of recession in 2000, the volatility reduced 2.540 and 2.396 for short-term and long-term investors. From the literature, it is understood that volatility is higher in times of recession and lower in periods of expansion (see Schwert 1989; Backus et al. 1992), which was not the case in the Malaysian stock market. However, the period of 1999–2000 entails the recovery period after the Asian financial crisis, hence; high volatility is to be expected as the market was still recovering. Moreover, the market volatility had reduced significantly from its preceding recession period from 5.526 to 3.095.

What is interesting is the lack of volatility in the veil of the global crisis. Share prices in Malaysia fell sharply in its aftermath, averaging 20% between 2007 and 2009 and Malaysia also suffered capital flight since mid-2008 with capital flows around 6 billion in 2009. The volatility in the denoised returns for the recession period of April 2008–May 2009 averaged 2.24 and in the short term 2.183, while the economy experienced its most significant drop in average growth of IP, averaging a -1.0042% growth rate for the recession period.

Nonetheless, the lack of severe impact can be explained as much of the shocks were absorbed by the domestic markets owing to abundant liquidity in the financial system, strong reserve position, sound banking system and had little collateral debt exposure to those originating in the US subprime market. Furthermore, drawing from their experiences in the Asian crisis, Malaysia had established broad-based financial sector reforms, which allowed them more resilience during this crisis. Hence, the restructuring of the financial sector paid off during the 2008 crisis and other recessions.

4.5.2 Indonesia

The year leading to the 1997 crisis was good for Indonesia; it was enjoying a boom cycle with low inflation, little volatility in stock markets (From Table 4.4, at only 2.6 for short-term traders and 1.48 for long-term investors), huge foreign reserves amounting to US$ 23 billion and well-functioning banking system. However, as the crisis hit Indonesia in June 1997, their stock exchange reached a historic low. Indonesia lost almost 13.5% of its GDP and its average IP growth plummeted to its lowest at –0.8575% on average. At the same time, the volatility for the short-term scale reached an average of 4.124 and 5.069 for the denoised returns.

With the help of the IMF bailout package, the economy began to recover slowly, and Indonesia enjoyed both stability in its business cycle

Table 4.4 Business cycle and volatility for Indonesia

		IP growth		*Stock volatility*	
		Average growth (%)	*Original*	*Short term*	*Denoised*
1990M03–1991M06	Boom	0.7746	103.421	1.944	2.649
1991M07–1993M12	**Recession**	**-0.5157**	**91.963**	**1.878**	**2.649**
1994M01–1995M03	Boom	0.7246	100.621	1.616	2.067
1995M04–1996M04	**Recession**	**-0.2499**	**95.504**	**1.702**	**1.827**
1996M05–1997M05	Boom	**0.3317**	99.400	2.600	1.48
1997M06–1998M09	**Recession**	**-0.8575**	**152.031**	**4.124**	**5.069**
1998M10–2000M10	Boom	0.4238	137.225	3.486	3.487
2000M11–2003M04	**Recession**	**-0.1439**	**117.565**	**2.64**	**2.543**
2003M05–2006M07	Boom	0.0809	112.309	2.439	2.103
2006M08–2007M08	**Recession**	**-0.4645**	**109.409**	**1.779**	**1.964**
2007M09–2008M08	Boom	0.8511	127.561	3.664	2.162
2008M09–2009M08	**Recession**	**-0.7571**	**143.051**	**4.135**	**4.641**
2009M09–2010M07	Boom	0.6376	113.807	1.787	1.347
2010M08–2014M12	**Recession**	**-0.1687**	**106.312**	**1.546**	**1.411**

and stock market until 2000. The recession that hit in November 2000 until April 2003 did not affect the stock market greatly, both short-term and long-term investors, who remained confident and less volatile until the global crisis of 2008. The highest peaks of volatility in the denoised and short term are seen in the Asian crisis followed by the global crisis.

Once again, in 2006 the Indonesian economy was plunged into recession, with its average growth rate at -0.4645% in the aftermath of the December 2004 tsunami. In 2005, the economy was able to stay afloat despite crumbling real wages, high inflation, rising unemployment and contracting consumer credit. The effects of which reared its ugly head in 2006 resulting in a credit crunch. Indonesia enjoyed one of its highest growths during the period of expansion in 2007 and 2008 before the global crisis hit. Its average IP growth rate was at 0.8511% and the volatility remained at bay at 3.664 and 2.162 respectively for short-term and denoised scales.

Following the crash in US capital markets, the Indonesian capital market had suspended for several days in October 2008 as its composite index went down for more than 10%. A rising perception amongst investors on the country risk because of global liquidity conditions caused investors to lose faith in the Indonesian stock exchange ensuing massive volatility in the short (4.135) and long run (4.641). This is further instigated by the quick withdrawal of foreign capital outflows.

Like Malaysia, Indonesia had two periods where volatility was higher in the boom period than in its subsequent bust period. The periods of January 1994–March 1995 (volatility was 2.067 and 1.827, respectively, for boom and bust periods) and October 1998–October 2000 (volatility was 3.487 and 2.543, respectively) stand as anomalies in the sample. Again, the lingering effects of the Asian financial crisis on the stock market can explain this during the 1998–end expansion period.

Malaysia and Indonesia were two countries in the sample severely affected by the Asian financial crisis, yet it is seen that the impact of the crisis was felt more sharply by Malaysia, the economy's growth fell on average by -0.9449% and the volatility spiked at 5.252 (short term) and 5.526 (long term). Whereas, the Indonesian economy fell by a lesser degree at 0.8575% and the volatility was also lower at 4.124 for short-term traders and 5.069 for long-term investors. However, in the reverberations of the crisis, the Malaysian stock market was able to recover more quickly, and to withstand better further crises than its neighbouring counterpart was.

4.5.3 Pakistan

The first recession in the sample was in 1992 as seen in Table 4.5, where interestingly, the volatility in the short run and long run remained lower than the period of expansion prior to this from 3.39 in the boom period to 2.84 in the bust period. This can be explained by fundamental liberalization of foreign exchange regime, investment controls were relaxed and incentives for domestic and foreign investments increased. One of the largest declines in the economy was seen in the recessionary period of 1994 until early 1996 at an average rate of -0.5194% but the volatility in the stock market remained low at 2.5 for short-term traders and 2.8 for long-term investors.

Proceeding further, Pakistan saw a stark decline in its economy in 1998 fuelled by its own debt crisis. While it was able to avert the Asian financial crisis, a turbulent political environment, and nuclear testing exacerbated the Pakistani economy and send it into a crisis. Owing to this debt crisis, the short-term scale shows great volatility, the highest denoised volatility for Pakistan, at 3.934 and short-term volatility at 3.631.

After which, the boom cycle of 1999–2000 did not show a significant change in pattern in volatility, the stock market remained volatile.

Table 4.5 Business cycle and volatility for Pakistan

		IP growth		*Stock volatility*	
		Average growth (%)	*Original*	*Short Term*	*Denoised*
1990M09–1992M11	Boom	0.0506	12.217	2.645	3.39
1992M12–1993M12	**Recession**	**-0.3325**	**10.648**	**1.944**	**2.842**
1994M01–1994M11	Boom	0.3899	12.146	2.112	1.755
1994M12–1996M02	**Recession**	**-0.5194**	**13.396**	**2.5**	**2.787**
1996M03–1998M05	Boom	0.3059	14.46	2.762	2.601
1998M06–1999M05	**Recession**	**-0.3552**	**20.655**	**3.934**	**3.631**
1999M06–2000M05	Boom	0.4392	17.381	3.43	3.472
2000M06–2002M12	**Recession**	**-0.3318**	**13.78**	**2.268**	**2.322**
2003M01–2005M06	Boom	0.3704	14.469	2.041	2.931
2005M07–2008M03	**Recession**	**-0.4435**	**13.256**	**1.895**	**2.066**
2008M04–2010M05	Boom	0.5791	14.695	3.068	3.566
2010M06–2011M04	**Recession**	**-0.3855**	**11.301**	**1.757**	**1.578**
2011M05–2012M03	Boom	0.4760	11.274	1.849	1.962
2012M04–2014M12	**Recession**	**-0.6446**	**9.17**	**0.988**	**1.285**

Following the debt crisis, Pakistan turned for aid from the Asian Development Bank, World Bank, Japan and the USA, while the IMF had sanctioned a short-term facility of US$ 300 million. This allowed the economic growth to pick up speed and trajectory and the stock market volatility remained at its highest for an expansionary period at 3.430 and 3.472 for the short-term and denoised scales, respectively. This is further explained by the influx of foreign investors and capital inflows to the stock market.

Yet again, Pakistan faced recession in 2000, which affected the long- and short-term volatility of its stock market, resultant of the dotcom crisis originating in the USA and the September 11 attacks in 2001 on the USA. Fearing Pakistan's involvement with the attacks, export orders of more than US$ 1 billion were cancelled immediately after the attacks propelling the economy into a recession. Interestingly, only the 1998 and 2000 crisis periods affected the volatility considerably, the other recession periods did not have as significant an impact as these two.

Pakistan's economic expansion of 2003–2005 had an effect on the long-term volatility of the stock market whereas short-term volatility remained low. The denoised return scale lingered at 3.472 from 3.631 from the previous recession. This can be explained by the influx of foreign capital inflows, culminating to around US$ 13.5 billion (for the expansion period). Pakistan had US$ 8.4 billion in foreign direct investments in 2006 and 2007 alone. An increase in foreign direct investment (FDI)'s while improving the long-term stability of the market, also caused short-term volatility in the market.

The global crisis affected Pakistan in an ongoing crisis from mid-2005 lasting up to mid-2008; remarkably, the crisis of 2007–2008 did not raise the volatility for both short-term traders and investors significantly. By the end of 2007, the market capitalization reached US$ 65.9 billion with 60 new Initial Public Offerings (IPOs) listed on the KSE, allowing for better stability in the crisis period. However, a significant decline in foreign investment in 2010, dropping by 54.6% caused the short-term investors to be more volatile at 1.76 than long-term investors at only 1.58.

Furthermore, in 2009 Pakistan received transmittals to the tune of US$ 7.8 billion with more than 70% of this money coming from the USA, Saudi Arabia, UAE and the UK. This allowed the economy to ascend to its strongest averaging at 0.5791% and caused the volatility to soar on average at 3.068 and 3.566 for the short-term and denoised scale returns, the highest for any expansionary period.

The Pakistani economy was most affected during the 1994 recession but its translation into the stock market did not result in the highest volatility peaks, as in the 1998 debt crisis. Hence, the stock market was affected by factors external to the economic growth.

4.5.4 *Turkey*

Another country plagued with much turbulence is Turkey; in the 1990s, Turkey witnessed several declines in the economy. The fundamental origins of these crises arose from the development of unsustainable domestic debt and an unstable financial sector. The 1991 Persian Gulf War shattered the Turkish economy following the UN embargo on Iraq ending the oil export routes from Turkey to Iraq. This rendered the Turkish stock market substantially volatile with an average volatility of 5.052 in short term and 3.977 in the long run. Even during the expansion period, owing to the ongoing war and instability, the stock market reported similar levels of volatility in the short- and long-run periods of 1990–1991 and 1991–1992.

The 1990s weathered another crisis in 1994 triggered mainly by inappropriate economic policies, which included a completely liberalized

Table 4.6 Business cycle and volatility for Turkey

		IP growth		*Stock volatility*	
		Average growth (%)	*Original*	*Short Term*	*Denoised*
1990M01–1991M01	Boom	0.5880	35.485	4.988	5.356
1991M02–1991M08	**Recession**	**-0.1003**	**29.468**	**5.052**	**3.977**
1991M09–1992M06	Boom	0.3838	28.572	4.886	5.049
1992M07–1993M10	**Recession**	**-1.0071**	**24.109**	**3.343**	**4.611**
1993M11–1994M10	Boom	0.6542	36.038	7.268	5.035
1994M11–1995M07	**Recession**	**-0.3431**	**23.481**	**3.574**	**4.127**
1995M08–1996M11	Boom	0.6724	22.677	4.122	3.493
1996M12–1998M07	**Recession**	**-0.4144**	**27.350**	**5.068**	**4.367**
1998M08–1999M07	Boom	0.7273	37.483	6.216	6.003
1999M08–2000M08	**Recession**	**-1.2574**	**30.637**	**5.161**	**5.305**
2000M09–2003M03	Boom	0.3939	31.861	4.697	4.398
2003M04–2004M03	**Recession**	**-0.4558**	**22.333**	**4.139**	**2.713**
2004M04–2006M12	Boom	0.3222	18.385	3.070	2.564
2007M01–2008M04	**Recession**	**-1.4320**	**20.247**	**2.759**	**2.096**
2008M05–2010M09	Boom	0.6838	35.485	4.988	5.356
2010M10–2014M12	**Recession**	**-0.3790**	**29.468**	**5.052**	**3.977**

capital account with no structural reforms to improve the fiscal situation after the crisis of 1991. Interestingly, the long-term returns showed a decrease in volatility from its previously growing economy (From Table 4.6, 5.35–3.98 in the long run). Furthermore, the growth phase of November 1993 until the start of the 1994 recession in October saw the highest short-term volatility throughout the sample period. This is a consequence of the Turkish stock market having its highest capitalization rate yet so far at US$ 37.8 billion.

The Turkish economy experienced its highest average growth during August 1998 until July 1999 at 0.7273%, which also translated into high volatility in the stock market for both short-term traders and long-term investors. Capital inflows to the tune of US$ 925 million and increase in official reserves amounting to US$ 811 million contributed to Turkey's growth. The short-term volatility was higher owing to an increase in short-term capital inflows by US$ 2.9 billion. Immediately after, the economy witnessed a stark decline, falling on average by -1.2574%, this came in tandem with the Russian crisis in mid-1998 and Brazilian crisis in 1999 where volatility remained on average at 5.2 for both short term and long term.

Faced with a multitude of crises, Turkey initiated to reform its financial structure with the commencement of the Banking Regulation and Supervision Agency and the Banking Sector Restructuring and Rehabilitation Programme, which was known as the Istanbul Approach to facilitate the strengthening of the financial sector. After which, the economy flourished and the stock market's volatility reduced significantly from previous periods.

Even though the Turkish economy was deeply affected from the 2008 global financial crisis, declining to an average of -1.432% for the period, owing mainly to its relation to the EU, the results show little volatility in response to it. Albeit, the Istanbul Stock Exchange had decreased by 54% in 2008 and experienced a sharp loss in FDIs and as there is a larger share of foreign investors than domestic, the exchange had suffered momentously in 2008.

However, the recovery was stronger than other emerging market. Unlike several EU countries that could not fulfil the Maastricht criteria, Turkey was able to owing to significant capital barriers after its 2000 banking crisis. It was only in 2011 that Turkey experienced a credit boom caused by easy domestic policies and global conditions. This caused large capital inflows and volatilities showed 2.67 and 2.072 for short-term and long-term scales.

Turkey, with its many crises followed by structural reforms and high capital inflows, experienced higher volatility during expansionary periods than in recessions. For long-term investors, Turkey had less volatility in the growth phase than recession only in the 1995–1996 growth period at 3.5 as compared to a 4.4 in the following recession of end-1996 until mid-1998. For short-term traders, the volatility remained higher throughout the expansionary phase of the economy. Overall, the Turkish stock market remained volatile throughout its sample period.

4.5.5 *Jordan*

The Jordanian capital market was without many events and remained relatively stable through the 22-year sample period. In the long-term scale, low volatility is seen throughout with the exception of 2005 from Table 4.7, which can be attributed to the crash of the ASE. At end-2005, the stock market had been overvalued and with exceptional and unprecedented performance, the share price index had reached an all-time high

Table 4.7 Business cycle turns and volatility for Jordan

		IP growth		*Stock volatility*	
		Average growth (%)	*Original*	*Short Term*	*Denoised*
1990M01–1991M03	Boom	1.0263	7.013	1.362	1.214
1991M04–1992M04	**Recession**	**-0.6288**	**6.05**	**0.849**	**1.202**
1992M05–1994M06	Boom	0.2188	8.118	1.614	1.366
1994M07–1995M11	**Recession**	**-0.6079**	**7.903**	**1.349**	**1.132**
1995M12–1996M11	Boom	0.7127	7.428	1.256	1.063
1996M12–1999M01	**Recession**	**-0.1175**	**7.611**	**1.214**	**1.152**
1999M02–2001M05	Boom	0.4083	7.253	1.161	1.035
2001M06–2002M07	**Recession**	**-1.4372**	**9.382**	**1.663**	**1.320**
2002M08–2004M12	Boom	0.4705	9.434	1.607	1.634
2005M01–2005M11	**Recession**	**-0.3620**	**14.012**	**2.222**	**3.887**
2005M12–2006M12	Boom	0.2672	13.154	2.006	1.606
2007M01–2009M09	**Recession**	**-0.1882**	**13.048**	**2.490**	**1.780**
2009M10–2014M01	Boom	0.1337	8.196	1.059	1.095

in November 2005 reaching 9,348 points. The economy was also negatively affected due to increasing oil prices in 2005 combined with a drop in external grants.

Several crises influenced the economy, starting from the Persian war and the drop in oil prices in 1991, Mexico's Tequila crisis of 1994, September 11 attacks on the USA, Iraq war in 2004 and the above-mentioned stock market crash in 2005, followed by the global financial crisis. However, from all of the crunches mentioned, the Jordanian economy took its deepest plunge in June 2001 until July 2002 averaged to be −1.4372% for the period. It is attributable mainly to the September 11 attacks on the USA and the decline in oil prices. However, the short-term and long-term volatility remained stable, with more volatility in the short run at 1.663. On the other hand, it is only in the boom cycle of 1994–1995, that volatility (1.34) in the denoised scale is higher than its following recession period (1.13), a consequence of the Mexican Tequila crisis.

In contrast, Jordan benefitted from the Iraq war, as there was a migration in capital from Iraq to Jordan in light of the war, causing the market to boom, and eventually crash in 2005. The 2008 crisis had a significant impact on the economy of Jordan with fluctuating oil prices but the stock market remained stable in the long run signifying that investors remained confident and took massive risks to stay in the market.

4.5.6 *Egypt*

The relationship between stock market volatility and business cycles in Egypt is rather interesting, as Egypt has been subject to several long recessions over the sample period of 1993–2014 as seen in Table 4.8, with results showing six recessions lasting on average 20 months per recession, with the longest being in January 2002 until February 2004. This was a difficult period for Egypt exacerbated by the September 11 attacks. The economic slowdown averaging at −0.8735% came from a drop in tourism, oil, the Suez Canal and regional security problems, but it was not the steepest downturn.

In the earlier stages of the sample period, Egypt was facing a major economic meltdown attributed to the Gulf war and a campaign of incidents that dissuaded tourism. Since the stock market was just reawakening in 1993, the impact of the economic situation on the stock market for short-term investors was minor but long-term investors experienced greater volatility at 2.507. It was after 1993, when liberalization took place, and tariffs were abolished did the economy start turning around. This is reflected in the Table 4.8, where during the expansion period of 1995 onwards, the volatility dropped significantly in the short and long run.

Table 4.8 Business cycle and volatility for Egypt

		IP growth		*Stock volatility*	
		Average growth	*Original*	*Short Term*	*Denoised*
1993M02–1995M02	**Recession**	**−0.5100**	**10.018**	**1.666**	**2.507**
1995M03–1996M01	Boom	0.9238	9.091	1.204	0.914
1996M02–1996M12	**Recession**	**−1.3014**	**7.443**	**1.225**	**1.607**
1997M01–1998M02	Boom	1.6558	11.837	2.067	3.163
1998M03–2000M03	**Recession**	**−1.1076**	**10.905**	**1.921**	**1.874**
2000M04–2001M12	Boom	1.2688	19.759	3.544	2.825
2002M01–2004M02	**Recession**	**−0.8735**	**14.336**	**2.550**	**2.222**
2004M03–2008M02	Boom	0.3642	15.225	3.036	2.760
2008M03–2009M04	**Recession**	**−1.7585**	**19.173**	**4.360**	**3.592**
2009M05–2010M08	Boom	1.4184	18.141	2.978	3.015
2010M09–2014M04	**Recession**	**−0.4207**	**14.814**	**2.318**	**2.431**

However, the volatility for the expansionary phase of 1997 (at 3.2 for denoised and 3.5 for short term) was much higher than the ensuing recession where the short-term and denoised returns averaged at 1.9. In the first quarter of 2000, a surge of consolidations took place in the cement and banking sectors driving up share prices. While this helped the economy grow, with liquidity tied up in the cement shares, the market began to fall, resulting in increased volatility in the long run (3.163). The decline in the market began in 2001 attributable to the global downturn, slow speed of privatization and political circumstances in the Middle East region. The effects of the September 11 attacks and declining oil prices further exacerbated this.

Egypt was severely impacted by the world food price crisis in 2008, which led to substantial increases in food price, and with high levels of poverty, the industrial production level of Egypt plummeted severely in 2008 to its lowest in the sample period at –1.7585%. The economy was in further turmoil as oil prices fell globally and as the crisis originating in USA started taking effect.

The Egyptian economy is heavily reliant on the USA for its export and was deeply affected by the crisis. The impact is visible on the stock market, with the short-term scale reading an average volatility of 4.360, and the denoised scales was at 3.592, the highest recorded. The Egyptian stock market saw a spike in short-term volatility as foreign investors hastened to sell their shares in the stock market as the news of the crisis became widespread.

4.5.7 Kuwait

From Table 4.9, it is assessed that investors had stable investments in the stock market, with low levels of volatility throughout the sample period. In recession periods, an increase in volatility was seen in 2001, right after the September 11 attack on the USA, which had caused panic amongst the traders and caused them to withdraw their money from the market.

However, this did not have any lasting effect on the stock market, as it did not affect the long-term volatility of the market, which remained low at 1.121. The highest short-term volatility was during the 2007–2009 global financial crisis. Owing to Kuwait's close linkages with global equity and credit markets, the crisis tightened liquidity conditions and affected investor confidences. Similarly,

Table 4.9 Business cycle and volatility for Kuwait

		IP growth		*Stock Volatility*	
		Average Growth (%)	*Original*	*Short term*	*Denoised*
1995M07–1996M04	**Recession**	**-0.0013**	**20.953**	**1.193**	**0.858**
1996M05–1997M05	Boom	0.6503	21.008	1.176	1.422
1997M06 1998M06	**Recession**	**-0.8780**	**20.785**	**1.339**	**1.131**
1998M07–1999M10	Boom	0.9284	20.71	1.473	1.337
1999M11–2001M04	**Recession**	**-1.0316**	**67.157**	**1.678**	**1.121**
2001M05–2005M02	Boom	0.2863	21.309	1.332	1.515
2005M03–2006M04	**Recession**	**-0.5563**	**21.010**	**1.507**	**1.959**
2006M05–2007M05	Boom	0.6726	20.932	1.715	1.576
2007M06–2009M04	**Recession**	**-0.5005**	**20.754**	**2.171**	**2.436**
2009M05–2010M12	Boom	0.6096	20.949	1.593	1.872
2011M01–2014M12	**Recession**	**-0.1869**	**17.845**	**1.743**	**1.673**

short-term traders were affected by 2011 crisis period with volatility averaging at 1.743, owing to an internal political crisis initiated through the Arab Spring.

For the denoised returns, in the long run the Kuwaiti stock market was affected mainly in the global financial crisis and its reverberations. Beginning in 2005, the Jordanian financial crisis had a significant impact on Kuwait and mainly affected the long-term investors, with volatility averaging at 0.1959%

Long-term volatility shot up in 2007–2008 in response to the global financial crisis. The reversal of speculative capital inflows in 2007 and 2008 had severely challenged the confidence of investors. At the same time, the Kuwaiti economy was struck with declines in oil prices and production, causing volatility to go up to 2.436. Similarly, in expansion periods, the only increase in volatility was seen in May 2009–December 2010, averaging 1.872 owing to a lack of global developments in equity markets.

Interestingly, Kuwait underwent six recessions, however, only the effect of the global economy crisis was felt substantially on the stock market. The other recessions did not seem to alter the state of the stock market by much. This can be explained by the strong position of domestic investors; there has always been sufficient money and confidence in the stock market, which was not affected by the economic conditions of Kuwaiti.

In contrast, higher volatility in denoised returns seen is in the boom phases of 1996 and 1998 at 1.422 and 1.337, respectively. Kuwait held its eighth parliamentary elections in 1996 and its ongoing retaliation with Iraq caused an increase in volatility in stock markets. The year 1998 saw the Operation Desert Thunder and Operation Desert Fox take place under which Kuwait was a coalition member.

4.5.8 *Nigeria*

The EGARCH analysis caused a loss of data for Nigeria, which resulted in the period to be limited until 2009 as seen in Table 4.10. Inimitably, the Nigerian stock market experienced more short-term volatility than it did in the long term. This is against the economic intuition that stock returns are less volatile over longer investment horizons (see Siegel 2008; Campbell and Viceira 2002).

It is only in 1998 that the volatility is higher in the expansion period by 3.38 in the denoised scales and 2.03 in the short term in relation to the following recession. The index started declining in 1998 continuing until 1999 from 6440.5 in 1997 to 5266.4 in 1999 caused by a series of upward adjustments in the minimum rediscount rate, which attracted funds away from the capital market.

Being another oil-rich country, Nigeria's economy soared in 2000s in response to higher oil prices, which contributes towards the increase in volatility in the short term. With more people investing in the stock market, the volatility of the stock market had increased. However, this was short-lived in 2002 as weaker oil prices and a subsequent revenue shortage

Table 4.10 Business cycle and volatility for Nigeria

		IP growth		*Stock volatility*	
		Average growth (%)	*Original*	*Short Term*	*Denoised*
1995M05–1996M02	**Recession**	**−0.2086**	**7.315**	**1.332**	**0.672**
1996M03–1997M02	Boom	0.3101	7.772	1.416	0.712
1997M03–1998M11	**Recession**	**−0.5717**	**9.183**	**1.972**	**1.201**
1998M12–2001M09	Boom	0.5675	11.750	3.836	2.028
2001M10–2005M01	**Recession**	**−0.4940**	**11.323**	**4.014**	**1.29**
2005M02–2006M11	Boom	0.6635	10.785	3.876	1.567
2006M12–2009M03	**Recession**	**−0.2922**	**14.006**	**6.000**	**2.417**

culminated into lower growth throwing the country into a recession until January 2005 lasting a total of 40 months. A spike in short-term volatility in 2002 was seen when oil prices started to fall initially.

The economy picked up once again in 2005 averaging at 0.6635%, when it won the approval of the Paris Club for a debt-relief deal to eliminate US$ 18 billion in debt for US$ 12 billion in payment and Nigeria was able to pay off its debt by 2006. During this period, the stock market remained stable during the long term. The denoised scales show an increase in volatility in response to the global economic crisis, in 2008 and 2009 owing to the volatile nature of crude oil prices.

4.5.9 *The UAE*

Table 4.11 shows us that the UAE market remained predictable throughout the sample period, with lower long-term variances in both phases of the business cycle with the exception of 2002 where it was higher in the expansion period (1.433) than the following recession (0.924) in 2003. The short-term scales show some capricious activity in 2001 a result of the September 11 attacks on the USA, which is also when the economy performed its worse averaging at -1.1448%.

Table 4.11 Business cycle and volatility for UAE

		IP growth		*Stock volatility*	
		Average growth (%)	*Original*	*Short term*	*Denoised*
1995M02–1996M01	**Recession**	**-0.1412**	**4.405**	**1.161**	**0.416**
1996M02–1998M06	Boom	0.2419	5.761	1.546	0.781
1998M07–1999M07	**Recession**	**-0.7018**	**6.58**	**1.849**	**0.829**
1999M08–2000M10	Boom	1.0097	6.117	1.720	1.001
2000M11–2002M04	**Recession**	**-1.1448**	**7.926**	**2.484**	**1.076**
2002M05–2003M05	Boom	0.9017	7.460	2.326	1.433
2003M06–2004M02	**Recession**	**-0.4355**	**7.145**	**2.042**	**0.924**
2004M03–2005M03	Boom	0.5290	7.589	2.011	0.847
2005M04–2007M02	**Recession**	**-0.2654**	**9.520**	**3.213**	**1.469**
2007M03–2008M03	Boom	0.8028	9.245	2.79	0.918
2008M04–2009M08	**Recession**	**-0.9981**	**10.972**	**3.459**	**1.465**
2009M09–2011M12	Boom	0.3217	11.383	2.782	1.470
2012M01–2014M12	**Receession**	**-0.115**	**12.45**	**2.89**	**2.10**

The main effect on the UAE stock market comes in conjunction with the global crisis, where volatility increased massively. UAE's stock markets were most affected by the global crisis, as the market capitalization declined from US$ 167.6 billion in 2006 to US$ 131.8 billion in 2008.

In 2009, Dubai had its own internal debt crisis resulting from an economic meltdown caused by the global financial crisis, which caused share prices to plummet. The global downturn had cautioned investor's capital preference causing much of the high-class projects in Dubai unable to attract buyers. Much of the effect on the economy came from plummeting oil prices worldwide. This caused the market to be highly volatile in the short run at 3.459.

Despite being subject to six recessions, the UAE economy remained fairly stable and this translated into a more stable stock market, with the exception of the global crisis and the internal debt crisis when stock market volatility increased significantly. However, the economy remained more stable as opposed to in 2000 when the economy on average declined by -1.1448% owing to the decline in world oil prices.

4.5.10 Saudi Arabia

In an event known as Riyadh's Black Monday, the Tadawul plunged 20% in 2006 causing the market to collapse. The volatility mainly bubbled from too much money being invested. As the country was enjoying its oil money, domestic investors chose to invest their money in the stock market causing it to become a bubble, which eventually burst. Apart from this anomaly, the volatility of the Saudi Arabian stock market remained stable in the short run throughout the period.

Interestingly, despite being an oil-dependent economy, the low oil prices in 1997 coupled with the East Asian crisis and increase in oil production by non-OPEC (Organization of the Petroleum Exporting Countries) countries, the stock market remained stable in the short run. While these did affect the economy of the country, sending Saudi Arabia into a recession from 1998 until 1999, the long-term investors were not deterred, as seen in Table 4.12. However, the volatility of the long-term scale in the denoised returns of 1999–2000 a period of expansion for Saudi Arabia was higher than the following recession, owing to the shifting prices of crude oil.

The global economic crisis brought down the world oil prices during the first and third quarter of 2009, which sent Saudi Arabia into another recession period lasting 14 months, the lowest average growth for the country at -1.0574% which resulted in the highest volatility spikes in both

Table 4.12 Business cycle and volatility for Saudi Arabia

		IP growth		*Stock volatility*	
		Average Growth (%)	*Original*	*Short term*	*Denoised*
1998M02–1999M07	**Recession**	**-0.4228**	**9.465**	**1.522**	**1.392**
1999M08–2000M11	Boom	0.7753	8.483	1.356	1.356
2000M12–2002M03	**Recession**	**-1.2381**	**7.663**	**1.281**	**0.978**
2002M04–2003M04	Boom	1.1294	11.229	1.78	2.194
2003M05–2004M01	**Recession**	**-0.5829**	**12.167**	**2.204**	**2.548**
2004M02–2005M02	Boom	0.7211	11.641	1.892	2.49
2005M03–2007M05	**Recession**	**-0.4949**	**20.25**	**3.224**	**3.381**
2007M06–2008M05	Boom	0.9798	14.441	2.427	2.367
2008M06–2009M07	**Recession**	**-1.0574**	**21.602**	**3.952**	**3.677**
2009M08–2012M03	Boom	0.5537	10.124	1.617	1.370
2012M04–2014M12	**Recession**	**-0.8015**	**9.639**	**1.704**	**1.428**

the short run and long run. This was quickly averted due to the exceptional surge in oil prices by 2009 allowing Saudi Arabia to absorb the negative impacts of the international financial crisis on its own economy.

The stock market was able to support itself despite the colossal ramification of the global crisis and oil prices, as the stock market was not open for foreign investors, hence while other countries experienced massive withdrawals from their markets, Saudi Arabia was safeguarded against that.

4.5.11 Qatar

The worse decline in Qatar's economy was witnessed in 2000–2002 where it fell by -1.31% on average owing to a decline in world oil prices in connection with the September 11 attacks in 2001, seen in Table 4.13. However, like Saudi Arabia, this did not transmute the stock market highly volatile; nonetheless, higher volatility is seen in the short run as compared to denoised returns as traders reacted swiftly to the news. Similarly, the largest volatility spikes come in connection with the global financial crisis but this did not result in a significant loss in the economy. Short-term and long-term investment showed a similar change in volatility at 4.4.

Interestingly, the denoised return's volatility spiked in 2004–2005 on average at 3.46, which is higher than the subsequent recession at 2.61

Table 4.13 Business cycle and volatility for Qatar

		IP growth		*Stock volatility*	
		Average Growth (%)	*Original*	*Short term*	*Denoised*
1998M02–1999M08	**Recession**	**-0.0738**	**26.485**	**2.401**	**1.291**
1999M09–2000M11	Boom	0.7206	32.950	1.208	0.701
2000M12–2002M03	**Recession**	**-1.3127**	**14.392**	**1.169**	**1.433**
2002M04–2003M07	Boom	1.0600	16.866	1.667	1.898
2003M08–2004M07	**Recession**	**-0.5552**	**17.572**	**2.561**	**2.991**
2004M08–2005M08	Boom	0.3017	22.507	2.367	3.463
2005M09–2007M03	**Recession**	**-0.2871**	**25.113**	**2.804**	**2.616**
2007M04–2008M04	Boom	0.7025	20.397	2.554	2.242
2008M05–2009M07	**Recession**	**-0.7891**	**30.570**	**4.387**	**4.399**
2009M08–2011M11	Boom	0.2774	21.144	2.260	1.568
2011M12–2014M12	**Recession**	**-0.0522**	**16.138**	**1.409**	**0.712**

following significant liberalization in its financial market in 2005. The liberalization included removing restriction on foreign participation in the market.

4.6 Conclusion

The objective of this chapter is to understand the relationship business cycles and stock market volatility has within the OIC member countries for short-term traders and long-term investors. To achieve this, a sample of 11 OIC member countries is selected where first, their business cycles using IP as a proxy is derived and second, the volatility of their daily stock market returns.

Running the data through EGARCH to obtain the volatility for the short-term (i.e. up to 8 days) and denoised returns (i.e. more than 32 days), allows for a clearer picture. The results showed that most of the countries, being oil rich and dependent, saw its business cycle and stock markets fluctuating owing to drops and increases in world oil prices. Saudi Arabia, UAE, Qatar, Nigeria, Kuwait are amongst some of the countries severely impacted by this.

Furthermore, all the countries in the sample were affected by the global crisis, some to a lesser extent than others. A contagion effect of the East Asian crisis was seen on Turkey, whereby in 1997 Turkey's stock market experienced high volatility as well and the economy went into recession. Pakistan, on the other hand, was able to withstand the effects of the crisis but also experienced a business cycle downfall due to its own internal problems.

An interesting observation from this study comes from the variegated results that are divergent from the classical believe that stock market volatility is lower in good times than in bad times. All sample countries had periods where the volatility was higher in the expansion period preceding the recession. However, these incongruities can be explained via economic or political events affecting the country, which did not affect the economy but caused undulations in the stock market.

References

Backus, D. K., Kehoe, P., & Kydland, F. E. (1992). Relative price movements in dynamic general equilibrium models of international trade (Working Paper No. 4243). Retrieved from Federal Reserve Bank of Cleveland: http://www.nber.org/papers/w4243.pdf.

Barro, R. J. (1989). New classical and keynesians, or the good guys and the bad guys. *Swiss Journal of Economics and Statistics*, *125*(III), 263–273.

Bernanke, B. S., & Gertler, M. (1995). Inside the black box: The credit channel of monetary policy transmission. *Journal of Economic Perspectives*, *9*(4), 27–48.

Campbell, J. Y., & Viceira, L. M. (2002). *Strategic asset allocation: Portfolio choice for long-term investors*. Oxford: Oxford University Press

Christiano, L. J., & Fitzgerald, T. J. (2003). The bandpass filter. *International Economic Review*, *44*(2), 435–465.

Hamilton, J. D., & Lin, G. (1996). Stock market volatility and the business cycle. *Journal of Applied Econometrics*, *11*(5), 573–593.

Mohseni-Cheraghlou, A. (2013). Islamic finance and financial inclusion: A case for poverty reduction in the Middle East and North Africa? Resource Document. World Bank. http://blogs.worldbank.org/allaboutfinance/islamic-finance-and-financial-inclusion-case-poverty-reduction-middle-east-and-north-africa. Accessed 2 July 2016.

Mun, H. W., Siong, E. C., & Thing, T. C. (2008). Stock market and economic growth in Malaysia: Causality test. *Asian Social Science*, *4*(4), 86–91.

Nelson, C. R., & Plosser, C. I. (1982). Trends and random walks in microeconomic time series, some evidence and implications. *Journal of Monetary Economics*, *10*(1), 139–162.

Nelson, D. B. (1991). Conditional Heteroskedasticity in asset returns: A new approach. *Econometrica*, *59*, 347–370

Schwert, G. W. (1989). Why does stock market volatility change over time?. *Journal of Finance*, *44*(5), 1115–1153.

Shirai, S. (2004). Testing the three roles of equity markets in developing countries: The case of China. *World Development, 32*(9), 1467–1486.

Siegel, J. J. (1991). The behaviour of stock returns around N.B.E.R. turning points: An overview (Working Paper No. 5–91). Retrieved from Weiss Centre Working Papers. http://finance.wharton.upenn.edu/weiss/.

Siegel, J. J. (2008). *Stocks for the long run.* 4th, New York: Mcgraw Hill

CHAPTER 5

Examining the Efficiency

Abstract As the primary role of the capital market is to allocate the economy's resources, the fundamental need for an efficient market arises from the importance of efficient resource allocations, which in turn will help the economy. In light of the efficient market hypothesis (EMH), several studies have been undertaken over the past two decade, but very few have been on the Organization of Islamic Cooperation (OIC). This chapter focuses on analysing the weak-form efficiency of OIC member stock markets to determine their efficiency rankings during different business cycles. The results are indicative of improving efficiency over the past decade.

Keywords Efficient market hypothesis · Weak-form efficiency · MFDFA · Efficiency ranking

5.1 Introduction

First introduced by Fama (1965), an efficient market is one in which prices fully reflect all available information. Fama discusses the concept of an efficient market and its importance, which was later conceptualized as the efficient market hypothesis (EMH). Accordingly, when a market is efficient, prices are random and thus a planned approach to investment cannot be successful. Consequently, investments patterns cannot be discerned and have to be based on risk taking. This underlines the importance of an

S. Arshad, *Stock Markets in Islamic Countries*, Palgrave CIBFR Studies in Islamic Finance, DOI 10.1007/978-3-319-47803-6_5

efficient market, that is, no investor or group of investors should be able to beat consistently the market by using a common investment strategy, which would allow them to gain profit every time.

As the primary role of the capital market is to allocate the economy's resources, the fundamental need for an efficient market arises from the importance of efficient resource allocations, which in turn will help the economy. Hence, allocative efficiency allows the public and private sectors to obtain funds for projects that will be most profitable, thereby stimulating economic growth. Therefore, for a market to be allocationally efficient, the market prices must truly reflect all available information and true transaction costs (Pesaran 2005).

Therefore, in line with the importance of an efficient market, this chapter analyses the efficiency of Organization of Islamic Cooperation (OIC) countries' stock markets individually during different business cycle turns to understand how the efficiency has changed for these countries over time.

5.2 Importance of Efficiency

Stock market efficiency becomes important to study as efficient stock markets forms the basis that would allow the optimal allocation of resources between those who have it and to those who need it. This in turn helps promote economic growth. As the central role of stock markets is to enhance mobilization of savings, the provision of equity capital to corporate sectors and to encourage efficient investment choices, it becomes necessary to ensure that the stock market achieves efficiency.

Furthermore, the importance of stock market efficiency lies in its benefits to policymakers in avoiding misallocation of resources that would have a negative impact on long-term economic growth. Improving the efficiency of resource allocation channels allows a reduction in distortions in an economy.

The significance of market efficiency can also be analysed from the point of view of an inefficient market. When a market is inefficient and prices do not fully reflect the true information, avenues are created for some investors to benefit more than others. As informational inefficiency arises, some investors would receive information on the market quicker than other investors and would be able to capitalize on this discrepancy. This can lead to substantial misallocation of resources that can have a negative impact on long-term economic growth.

5.3 Stock Market Efficiency in the OIC

When discussing the market efficiency of developing and emerging markets, a common factor amongst these countries is that they have taken the step to liberalize their capital markets to ensure economic growth, by opening up stock markets to foreign ownership. It is contended that with liberalization, emerging stock markets become more attractive to foreign investors for portfolio diversification, and are able to increase liquidity and informational transparency leading to higher degrees of efficiency. Hence, as the EMH postulates that as markets becomes more open and transparent, the price of its assets would reflect the newly available information and ultimately be more efficiently valued. Moreover, with financial liberalization, the increase in international risk sharing reduced equity premium and cost of capital, allowing markets to be more efficient. These studies signify the importance of market liberalization to emerging countries. The emerging markets studied have all liberalized their markets at one point or other, changing the dynamics of their respective markets and consequently altering its efficiency.

The past literature suggest that stock markets in Islamic countries, both in Middle East–North Africa (MENA) and Asia, are smaller, more volatile, less liquid and more prone to higher risk premium, higher cost of funds and poor legal and governance framework as compared to efficient stock markets found in developed countries. The above inefficiencies are often attributed too poor quality of information channels, high trading cost, disintermediation and low trading activity due to investment barriers, owing to protectionism and less integration with world markets (Rizvi et al. 2014). With the increasing interest in the OIC, there needs to be better infrastructural grounds for the markets to actively accept and process these investments. Hence, there becomes an urgent need to analyse the stock market's efficiency in the event of increasing foreign direct investments (FDIs) into the markets.

5.4 Theory Behind Efficient Markets

First introduced by Fama (1965), the EMH has been subjected to many theoretical and empirical tests. EMH proposed that securities markets were extremely efficient in reflecting information about individual stocks and the market as a whole. Fama defined it as, 'A market where there are large numbers of rational, profit-maximizers actively competing, with each trying to predict future market values of individual securities, and where important current information is almost freely available to all participants…'.

Other definitions of market efficiency were given by Jensen (1978), who states, 'A market is efficient with respect to information set Ω_t if it is impossible to make economic profits by trading on the basis of information set Ω_t'. Malkiel (1992) (Efficient Market Hypothesis, New Palgrave Dictionary of Money and Finance) provided a rather similar definition:

> A capital market is said to be efficient if it fully and correctly reflects all relevant information in determining security prices. Formally, the market is said to be efficient with respect to some information set, Xt, if security prices would be unaffected by revealing that information to all participants. Moreover, efficiency with respect to an information set, Ω_t, implies that it is impossible to make economic profits by trading on the basis of Ω_t.

The underlying concept of EMH was first introduced by Samuelson (1965) who in his seminal paper birthed the idea through his interest in temporal pricing models of storable commodities that are harvested and subjected to decay. Samuelson noted that if a market is informationally efficient, any changes in price, if properly anticipated, should be unforecastable. In other words, the prices would include all the information and expectations of all market participants. Fama's approach to the EMH is summarized in the axiom 'prices fully reflect all available information'.

The hypothesis finds its basis in the random walk hypothesis (RWH) and martingale model, which are two statistical descriptions of unforecastable changes in price (Blume and Durlauf 2007). Primarily, the logic behind the RWH relies on the fact that the flow of information is unconstrained and will be reflected immediately in stock prices. Hence, tomorrow's price change would only reflect tomorrow's news and would be independent from any price changes today.

However, news is often unpredictable and thus the resulting price change must be unpredictable and random. Thus, the price would reflect fully all known information. Economists stress the importance of assessing the informational efficiency in the market, as when a market is efficient, investors are able to determine the risk and returns for their investments because there would be no undervaluation or overvaluation for their asset.

At its core, the EMH follows three basic premises as outlined by Pesaran (2005): First, investor rationality: EMH operates under the assumption that investors are rational, in the sense that they are able to react correctly when faced with new information. Second, arbitrage: each individual investment decision and trade decisions made are so that it satisfies the law of arbitrage. Third, collective rationality: the random errors of investors tend to cancel each other out in the market. However, this requires individual errors to be cross-sectionally independent.

Furthermore, Fama classified EMH into three different forms of efficiency, namely, weak form efficiency, semi-strong form efficiency and strong form efficiency. The weak form of the EMH takes the information contained in the past price history solely as its information, whereas the semi-strong form takes all information that is publicly available at that time, which includes both present and past history of prices (making the weak form a restriction of this). Lastly, the strong form of EMH takes into account all information known to anyone at that time.

The weak-form EMH stresses that stock prices already reflect all the information that can be obtained from the market, such as past data, trading volume or short interest, implying that trend analysis would be redundant. This form of hypothesis holds that if information such as past stock price data conveyed reliable signals about future performances, all investors would be exploiting these signals, negating their value in the end as it becomes popular. For instance, a buy signal would signal an immediate price increase, as everyone in the market would have learned to exploit the signals.

Subsequently, the semi-strong form of EMH states that information that can be obtained publically must already be emulated in the stock price. Such information could include past prices, fundamental data on the firm's product line, quality of management, balance sheet composition, patents held, earnings forecasts, accounting practices and so on.

Finally, the strong-form EMH states that the stock prices reflect all that is relevant to the firm, including information that would only be available to company insiders. This is an extreme form of EMH, with many scholars questioning its validity. The proposition that information is available to corporate officials before public allows them to profit from that information, whereas the Securities and Exchange Commission is directed mainly to prevent this from happening. Fama had regarded the strong form version as a benchmark against which other forms of market efficiencies would be judged.

5.5 Data and Methodology

The data and country selection are the same as Chapter 4. However, to maintain uniformity in data analysis, the data set for this chapter is limited to 1998–2014. To avoid reiteration of information, the data set and methodology for business cycles are not discussed here and can be found in Section 4.3.

5.5.1 Testing Market Efficiency

Testing for market efficiency has garnered enormous attention over the past several decades. According to Fama (1990), tests of market efficiency often focus on whether the specific investment or stock earns excess returns, with some tests taking into account transaction cost and execution feasibility. When there is evidence of excess returns in a test of market efficiency, it indicates that markets are inefficient.

Earlier tests focused on short-horizon returns (i.e. within 1-year holding periods) under the presumption that the expected rate of return is constant through time. These test held that if realized returns were serially uncorrelated, the markets were efficient. However, as most modern asset pricing theories involve a direct mean–variance trade-off, testing for efficiency has evolved to include modelling the time variation. In which, developments such as ARCH, GARCH time series models have been made.

The traditional approach to arguing for weak-form efficiency is return independence, often measured by correlation. However, this is mainly suitable for developed securities markets, which assume that the prices are not exposed to substantial upward trends and are more liquid. More dynamic time series models include autoregression models, ARIMA model and time series regression models.

Furthermore, there are several methodologies in the literature apart from finance and economic models, to measure the degree of efficiency. Typical methods include probability distribution functions, correlation functions and network analysis. Amongst these, the distribution function is most intensively researched. However, another popular method is the Detrended Fluctuation Analysis (DFA) derived from econophysics, proposed by Peng et al. (1685–1689) who based their proposed methods on a plethora of evidence that finds stock market data to be multifractal in nature.[1]

Based on the multifractal nature of stock market, this chapter uses the proposed methodology of Peng et al. (1685–1689); Multifractal Fluctuation

Detrended Fluctuation Analysis (MFDFA). The MFDFA is often used to analyse long-range autocorrelations and describe the fractal properties. The MFDFA comprises the Hurst exponents, which describe the dimensions of multifractals. The Hurst exponent is related to the predictability of the time series. If the market is efficient, its return must follow random walk behaviour, hence it is unpredictable. Therefore, the Hurst exponent can be used to measure market efficiency (see Cajuerio et al. 2009).

The MFDFA identifies the efficiency ranking and enables the readers to know the extent of inefficiency. The rationale behind relying on MFDFA is owing to the nature of stock market data, which has been argued to be multifractal in nature. Rizvi et al. (2014), has shown the stock market data across emerging countries and developed countries exhibit long memory process which can be decomposed using this method. Prior researches have shown evidences of structural differences in emerging markets, which covers the sample countries of this chapter (see Rizvi et al. 2014). Kantelhardt et al. (2002) provided the complete technical details of MFDFA.

5.6 Empirical Analysis

The empirical analysis is subdivided into three sections for a better and conclusive understanding of stock market efficiency in the OIC. First, the OIC sample member countries is analysed over the complete time period, that is, 1998–2014. Second, the efficiency of sample countries is found in response to three segmented time periods, covering the Asian financial crisis (1998–1999), the dotcom crisis and the September 11 attacks (2000–2002) and global economic crisis (2008–2010), to analyse the efficiency during recession periods.

Lastly, with the unique business cycle of each country, this chapter analyses the efficiency of its stock market in juxtaposition. In regards to the theory outlined in earlier sections, for a market to be efficient, any form of fluctuations should assume random walk behaviour. This interprets into $h(q)$'s related to different q's are equal to 0.5. In this analysis, the focus is on both large and small fluctuations, and hence defines market efficiency measure as:

$$D = \frac{1}{2}\left(|h(-4) - 0.5| + |h(4) - 0.5|\right) \quad (5.1)$$

In Eq. 5.1 above, scale exponents of h(−4) and h(4) are used for symbolizing the small and large price fluctuations. To be efficient, the market has to have a value of *D* close to 0. In other words, a large value of efficiency indicates a less efficient market.

5.6.1 Overall Efficiency

From Table 5.1, it can be noted that the overall efficiency to vary across countries for short and long term. In the short term, Turkey appears to be most efficient throughout the sample period, while Egypt being the least efficient market. However in the long term, Turkey declines to second place and Kuwait is least efficient in long term. Turkey's position as the most efficient stock market is in line with the development stage of the market, that is, by volume, market capitalization and a stable economy.

Similarly, Egypt remains at the lower end of the spectrum owing mainly to its economic and political stability, which reflected higher volatility in the stock market. Throughout, events such as the September 11 attacks, the global financial crisis and the Arab Spring have had catastrophic implications for the Egyptian stock market leading to higher levels of inefficiency.

A possibility of biased ranking may exists owing to the length of the sample period. As over 14 years, several factors or circumstances may lead to a more volatile nature in one market over another. For instance, it is interesting to note that overall Indonesia showed greater efficiency than

Table 5.1 Overall period efficiency ranking (in descending order)

1998–2014			
Short-term		*Long-term*	
1. Turkey	0.1206	1. Saudi Arabia	0.0673
2. Indonesia	0.1302	2. Turkey	0.0952
3. Nigeria	0.1372	3. Qatar	0.0985
4. Saudi Arabia	0.1791	4. Indonesia	0.1170
5. Jordan	0.1859	5. Malaysia	0.1485
6. Malaysia	0.2319	6. Pakistan	0.1564
7. Qatar	0.6868	7. Nigeria	0.1573
8. UAE	0.7172	8. Egypt	0.1934
9. Kuwait	1.0183	9. Jordan	0.2199
10. Pakistan	5.2185	10. UAE	0.3253
11. Egypt	11.4055	11. Kuwait	0.4896

Malaysia for both short- term and long term. The overall efficiency of Indonesia may be attributable to the fast recovery and proinvestment policies of the government over the last 5 years. Looking deeper into the market, Indonesia faced an increase in liquidity, which may have contributed towards improving efficiency of the market in the short term.

5.6.2 *Ranking of Markets for Major Periods*

An overall efficiency ranking may bring forth inaccurate results and interpretations owing to many significant events clubbed into one period. Hence, for a further understanding of the efficient, considering the history of stock markets over the past decade, three distinct phases can be observed in the global markets and in particular those affecting OIC member countries.

The first regime is the Asian financial crisis, which affects several of the sample countries, directly and indirectly. The second regime is the 2000–2002 crises, marred by accounting scandals, like Enron, WorldCom and the dotcom crisis. Further, this period also saw the September 11 attacks on the USA bringing the US markets to a halt. The third distinct phase is the 2008–2010 global economic crisis, which brought several economies to a near standstill (See Table 5.2).

Interestingly, while this period focuses particularly on the Asian financial crisis, the two countries affected directly, that is, Malaysia and Indonesia seem to have performed better than other OIC member countries, owing mainly to the development stage of the markets. Post-crisis,

Table 5.2 Efficiency ranking from 1998–1999 (in descending order)

1998–1999 Recession phase			
Short-term		*Long-term*	
1. Nigeria	0.0809	1. Kuwait	0.0571
2. Qatar	0.0920	2. Egypt	0.0952
3. Saudi Arabia	0.1042	3. Qatar	0.0969
4. Malaysia	0.1648	4. Jordan	0.0999
5. Pakistan	0.1902	5. Saudi Arabia	0.1078
6. Turkey	0.2153	6. Indonesia	0.1256
7. Jordan	0.2392	7. Turkey	0.1311
8. Indonesia	0.2587	8. Nigeria	0.1438
9. UAE	0.2993	9. Pakistan	0.1915
10. Egypt	0.3753	10. Malaysia	0.4588
11. Kuwait	0.3795	11. UAE	0.5164

the Malaysian stock markets managed to stabilize more effectively than Indonesia in the short term. However, in the long run, Indonesia outranks Malaysia in terms of efficiency, in relation to the International Monetary Fund (IMF) bailout package it received post-crisis.

Egypt displays variegated levels of efficiency for short term and long term. In the short run, it ranked at the lower end of the range caused by highly volatile market, which was full of frictions in the trading process with limited provision of information to market participants, impaired further by limited financial intermediaries. This caused an increase in short-term volatility and hence reducing its efficiency. However, it was also in this period that Egypt was enjoying an economic boom and the market was able to recover in the long term when the market started shifting from traditional 'value stocks' to new-economy 'growth stocks'.

Moving on, looking at the next major global condition, the 2001–2002 period was marked with several unfortunate events as seen in Table 5.3. The dotcom crisis, the September 11 attacks are amongst some of the events affecting the sample countries. The worst decline in Qatar's economy was witnessed in this regime phase owing to the decline in world oil prices in conjunction with the September 2001 attacks causing massive amounts of volatility in the stock markets. Similarly, most of the oil-dependent economies suffered during this phase as oil prices soared and investors quickly withdrew their investments from Muslim countries.

Like Qatar, Kuwait suffered from a quick withdrawal of money from the markets after the September 11 attacks and owing to Kuwait's close

Table 5.3 Efficiency ranking from 2001–2002 (in descending order)

2001–2002 Recession phase			
Short-term		*Long-term*	
1. Turkey	0.1352	1. Indonesia	0.0824
2. Pakistan	0.1443	2. Egypt	0.1017
3. Malaysia	0.1609	3. Turkey	0.1355
4. Egypt	0.1626	4. Malaysia	0.1495
5. Jordan	0.1651	5. Jordan	0.1595
6. Nigeria	0.1821	6. Saudi Arabia	0.1620
7. Saudi Arabia	0.2019	7. Nigeria	0.1622
8. UAE	0.2268	8. UAE	0.1689
9. Indonesia	0.2921	9. Pakistan	0.1851
10. Qatar	0.4538	10. Qatar	0.2267
11.Kuwait	0.4552	11. Kuwait	0.4733

linkages with global equity and credit markets, the crisis tightened liquidity conditions and affected investor confidences. On the other hand, Turkey's economy was enjoying a boom and its stock market enjoyed the effects from a reform of its financial structure with the commencement of the Banking Regulation and Supervision Agency and the Banking Sector Restructuring and Rehabilitation Programme.

Pakistan, however, sees a stark difference in efficiency ranking for short and long term. Before the dotcom crisis and the September 11 attacks affected Pakistan, aids from the Asian Development Bank, World Bank, Japan and the USA allowed the economy to pick up speed and stock markets remained stable and more efficient. However, in the long run, after the effect of the crises, Pakistan's stock market suffered greatly, like several other Muslim-dominant nations with strong economic ties with the USA.

In 2000, a wave of consolidation took place in the cement and banking sectors of Egypt, driving up share prices and therefore making the market more efficient. This also explains the lower efficiency in the short term than in the long term. As share prices started rising, particularly in the cement sector, liquidity was tied up in cement shares causing other stocks to suffer and this eventually led to the market dropping.

Table 5.4 ranks the sample member countries during the 2008–2010 period, coloured by the global economic crisis mainly. Malaysia was able to maintain its efficiency owing to abundant liquidity in the financial system, a strong reserve positing and little collateral debt exposure to the US subprime market. Most of the negative effect on the stock market

Table 5.4 Efficiency ranking from 2008–2010 (in descending order)

2008–2010 Recession phase			
Short-term		*Long-term*	
1. UAE	0.1044	1. Qatar	0.0855
2. Malaysia	0.1382	2. Saudi Arabia	0.1006
3. Indonesia	0.1433	3. Turkey	0.1228
4. Egypt	0.1599	4. UAE	0.1476
5. Kuwait	0.1705	5. Malaysia	0.1714
6. Jordan	0.1844	6. Pakistan	0.1924
7. Turkey	0.2077	7. Indonesia	0.2008
8. Saudi Arabia	0.2332	8. Egypt	0.2073
9. Qatar	0.2497	9. Nigeria	0.2279
10. Nigeria	0.3358	10. Kuwait	0.2870
11. Pakistan	5.2226	11. Jordan	0.3114

during period can be attributed to the fluctuating oil prices, as many OIC member countries are oil-dependent economies; any vacillation in oil prices causes the market's volatility to shift.

Owing to Kuwait's close linkages with global equity and credit markets, the crisis tightened liquidity conditions and affected investor confidences, causing the efficiency to fall significantly from previous periods. Similarly, the reversal of speculative capital inflows in 2007 and 2008 had severely challenged the confidence of investors. At the same time, the Kuwaiti economy was struck with declines in oil prices and production.

5.6.3 Efficiency Rankings of Individual Markets

This section will look into individual markets, analysing its market efficiency against the country's business cycle. Based on this, the efficiency measure for the sample countries provides interesting insight for the sample countries. Economic upswings and financial liberalizing policies positively influence efficiency. Cajueiro et al. (2009) explored and deduced a positive impact of financial liberalization on the market efficiency in Greece.

Malaysia

From Table 5.5, it is seen that efficiency is lower in boom period than its preceding recessionary period of the Asian financial crisis. While this goes against the contemporary literature, it can be explained by a lower level of efficiency after the crisis, as the markets were still recovering and further, the Malaysian government took to implementing capital controls and fixing the exchange rate regime, thus affecting the investor's sentiment in the financial markets. Furthermore, illiquidity in the Malaysian market caused inefficiency in the market.

An interesting observation is the increase in inefficiency for long-term investors for the 1998 recessionary period. This may be attributed to volatility and increasing number of retail and shorter horizon investors. A surge in shorter horizon investor base, may increase the efficiency in the short term, whereas may adversely affect the long-term efficiency. From the table above, in the cases of the 2008 and 2010 recessionary periods, the markets were more efficient during recession phases than its following boom periods. This again, can be explained by the recovering market post-global financial crisis of 2008.

Table 5.5 Business cycles and efficiency for Malaysia

		Efficiency	
		Short term	*Long term*
1998M01–1998M12	**Recession**	**0.1631**	**0.5218**
1999M01–2000M08	Boom	0.2167	0.2570
2000M09–2002M01	**Recession**	**0.1946**	**0.1053**
2002M02–2004M06	Boom	0.1393	0.0403
2004M07–2005M06	**Recession**	**0.1649**	**0.1073**
2005M07–2006M06	Boom	0.1202	0.0361
2006M07–2007M03	**Recession**	**0.1355**	**0.3388**
2007M04–2008M03	Boom	0.0056	0.2639
2008M04–2009M5	**Recession**	**0.1467**	**0.0454**
2009M06–2010M06	Boom	0.1661	0.1743
2010M07–2011M03	**Recession**	**0.0677**	**0.1148**
2011M04–2014M12	Boom	0.1184	0.0505

In the short term, the Malaysian market was most efficient during the 2007–2008 expansion period owing to abundant liquidity in the financial system, strong reserve position, sound-banking system. Malaysian stock market remained highly efficient in 2005, a year that saw the abandonment of the fixed exchange regime, in the long term. This change in fundamental affected the long term more than it did during the short term.

Indonesia

Indonesia, being the only other country in the sample to be greatly affected by the Asian financial crisis, saw significant volatility in stock markets causing inefficiencies. From Table 5.6, the market was most inefficient during the Asian financial crisis in the short run at 0.33 and at 0.32 in the long run. During the crisis, the Indonesian stock market had reached a historic low, and its economy lost almost 13.5% of its GDP, hence the significant inefficiency in the stock market.

In the recessionary period of 2006–2007, efficiency was higher than in the following boom phase. This can be explained by the increase in volatility after the credit crunch Indonesia experienced in 2006. In the concurrent boom period, (2007–2008) Indonesia enjoyed one of its highest growth periods, which led to an increase in short-term activity and speculation thus increasing volatility significantly. It is interesting to note that Indonesia was most efficient in the short term during the 2010–2014

Table 5.6 Business cycles and efficiency for Indonesia

		Efficiency	
		Short term	*Long term*
1998M01–1998M10	**Recession**	0.3307	0.3166
1998M10–2000M10	Boom	0.2676	0.1278
2000M11–2003M04	**Recession**	0.1495	0.1951
2003M05–2006M07	Boom	0.1188	0.1143
2006M09–2007M08	**Recession**	0.1467	0.3323
2007M09–2008M08	Boom	0.1638	0.1621
2008M09–2009M08	**Recession**	0.1937	0.3371
2009M09–2010M07	Boom	0.1684	0.0949
2010M08–2014M12	**Recession**	0.1120	0.1543

recession at 0.11, significantly lower than its efficiency during the Asian financial crisis. Similarly, in the long term, it was most efficient during 2009–2010. The 2008 crisis had an adverse effect in Indonesian markets as its composite index went down more than 20% and country risk increased for investors owing to worsening global liquidity conditions.

Hence, for both Malaysia and Indonesia, post-Asian financial crisis, structural and financial reformation to their stock markets allowed then better stability and greater efficiency during the global economic crisis.

Pakistan

The efficiency of the stock during the boom period of 1999 was significantly lower than during its preceding recessionary period of 1998. This was owing to the monetary assistance received from the Asian Development Bank, World Bank, Japan, the USA and an IMF sanctioned short-term facility of US$ 300. This sudden surge in the stock market caused greater volatility than the previous debt crisis of 1998.

However, the same is not true for the long term, indicating that an internal debt crisis and contagion effects of the Asian financial crisis had fundamentally affected the market, causing more impact on long-term investors than short-term traders.

Another important event, is the 2008–2010 phase, while this is marked as a business cycle boom, the stock market was highly inefficient at 8.22 in the short term as in Table 5.7. However, this is considered an anomaly in the data, and is rejected. Nonetheless, in 2009, the economy

Table 5.7 Business cycles and efficiency for Pakistan

		Efficiency	
		Short term	*Long term*
1998M06–1999M05	**Recession**	0.0949	0.3141
1999M06–2000M05	Boom	0.2455	0.1826
2000M06–2002M12	**Recession**	0.1589	0.0873
2003M01–2005M06	Boom	0.2580	0.2801
2005M07–2008M03	**Recession**	0.1867	0.0608
2008M04–2010M05	Boom	8.2195	0.1756
2010M06–2011M04	**Recession**	0.0230	0.2358
2011M05–2012M03	Boom	0.0680	0.4798
2012M04–2014M12	**Recession**	0.0818	0.1248

was insulated with transmittals to the tune of US$ 7.8 billion, causing volatility to soar significantly Pakistan suffered from a decline in foreign investment causing short-term volatility to increase.

Turkey

The Turkish market was least efficient during the 1998 recession period at 0.23 owing to a higher volatility in the stock market coming from capital inflows to the tune of US$ 925 million. The short term had lower efficiency than long term, at this period, as there was an increase in short-term capital inflows by US$ 2.9 billion. Similarly, the long-term efficiency was lowest during the 1999–2000 recession at 0.33. It was during this phase, that Turkey saw a stark decline in its economy, this came in tandem with the Russian crisis in mid-1998 and Brazilian crisis in 1999, which had severe effects on the Turkish economy and stock market.

On the other hand, Turkey was most efficient in the long term during 2007–2008 as seen in Table 5.8, which interestingly was a recession. However, the increase in efficiency can be explained by the reform structure Turkey established during this period. Turkey initiated to reform its financial structure with the commencement of the Banking Regulation and Supervision Agency and the Banking Sector Restructuring and Rehabilitation Programme, which was known as the Istanbul Approach to facilitate the strengthening of the financial sector. After which, the economy flourished and the stock market's efficiency increased significantly from previous periods (in the long run, it decreased by 0.04).

Table 5.8 Business cycles and efficiency for Turkey

		Efficiency	
		Short term	*Long term*
1998M1–1998M12	**Recession**	**0.2345**	**0.1124**
1999M01–1999M07	Boom	0.1204	0.1817
1999M08–2000M08	**Recession**	**0.1432**	**0.3347**
2000M09–2003M03	Boom	0.1169	0.1183
2003M04–2004M03	**Recession**	**0.1035**	**0.1652**
2004M04–2006M12	Boom	0.0594	0.1255
2007M01–2008M04	**Recession**	**0.1344**	**0.0848**
2008M05–2010M09	Boom	0.1478	0.1045
2010M10–2014M12	**Recession**	**0.137**	**0.1260**

Jordan

Table 5.9 outlines the business cycle dates and efficiency values for Jordon. Interestingly, the Jordanian market was most efficient post-global crisis, during the 2009–2010 economic boom, for short-term investors. The massive confidence investors had in the Jordanian market, as investors choose to stay in the market can explain this.

Another interesting observation is the efficiency during the 2005 stock market crash, whereby in the long run it was efficient at 0.158 and in the short term at 0.192. This affected the stock market efficiency to a lesser degree than the 2008 financial crisis. The fluctuating oil prices had a significant impact on the stock market, particularly for the long run.

Table 5.9 Business cycles and efficiency for Jordan

		Efficiency	
		Short term	*Long term*
1998M01–1999M1	**Recession**	0.2561	0.1784
1999M02–2001M05	Boom	0.1917	0.0469
2001M06–2002M07	**Recession**	0.1444	0.1408
2002M08–2004M12	Boom	0.2208	0.3777
2005M01–2005M11	**Recession**	0.1338	0.2013
2005M12–2006M12	Boom	0.1921	0.1579
2007M01–2009M09	**Recession**	0.2080	0.4357
2009M10–2014M01	Boom	0.1164	0.1141

Egypt
For the Egyptian market, it was more efficient during the boom phase of 2000–2001 than the following recession, going against intuition. However, this can be explained by the increase in volatility in the stock market, as this period was full of frictions in the trading process with limited provision of information to market participants, impaired further by limited financial intermediaries.

Interestingly, the market was most efficient in the 2009–2010 post-recession phase, as shown in Table 5.10, at only 0.05 for short term, which goes against intuition, as the Egyptian economy was heavily reliant on the USA for its exports and was deeply affected by the crisis. However, as the Egyptian financial sector in the global arena is still limited, the stock market was able to sustain itself during this period. Meanwhile, in the long term, the stock market remained most efficient during the 2004–2008 boom at 0.07.

It was during this period, Egypt underwent massive reformation of its banking system, which encouraged mergers to create strong banking entities. The reformations further increased liquidity in the market, and reliance on securities and mortgage investments was limited.

Kuwait
The period of 2009–2010 records the highest efficiency for the Kuwaiti market in the short term and during 2001–2005 for long term. Both of these periods were economic expansions where the economy was rising significantly, allowing the stock market to flourish expressively.

On the other hand, intense inefficiency is noticed in Table 5.11, during an expansionary phase (2001–2005) at 11.67, which is considered anomaly, as in MFDFA, anything above one is considered an error. Therefore,

Table 5.10 Business cycles and efficiency for Egypt

		Efficiency	
		Short term	*Long term*
1998M03–2000M03	**Recession**	**0.3357**	**0.2134**
2000M04–2001M12	Boom	0.2107	0.1760
2002M01–2004M02	**Recession**	**0.2345**	**0.1727**
2004M03–2008M02	Boom	0.0713	0.0343
2008M03–2009M04	**Recession**	**0.1448**	**0.2064**
2009M05–2010M08	Boom	0.0498	0.1981
2010M09–2014M04	**Recession**	**0.1449**	**0.2064**

Table 5.11 Business cycles and efficiency for Kuwait

		Efficiency	
		Short term	*Long term*
1998M07–1999M10	Boom	0.0872	0.8212
1999M11–2001M04	**Recession**	**0.4448**	**0.5244**
2001M05–2005M02	Boom	11.6700	0.0949
2005M03–2006M04	**Recession**	**0.1203**	**0.1494**
2006M05–2007M05	Boom	0.1717	0.2460
2007M06–2009M04	**Recession**	**0.1716**	**0.1526**
2009M05–2010M12	Boom	0.0511	0.2325
2011M01–2014M12	**Recession**	**0.1551**	**0.1609**

Kuwait was least efficient during the 1998–2001 phase for the short run and long run, owing mainly to the political instability plaguing Kuwait at that time. The previous year saw the Operation Desert Thunder and Operation Desert Fox take place under which Kuwait was a coalition member.

UAE

Table 5.12 shows that the UAE stock market was most efficient during the 2008–2009 recessionary phase during the short term while the market was least efficient in the long term at 0.362. The UAE market had close links with the US markets, and faced portfolio losses of up to 42%. The Dubai debt crisis further affected the market in 2009.

As the economy plunged into a recession in 2002, the short term showed highest inefficiency at 0.32. Greater inefficiency during this period, is reflected in the low level of FDIs received as opposed to its expected attractiveness. Furthermore, it was still recovering from the 2001 crisis and global oil price fluctuations.

Nigeria

As seen in Table 5.13, the data for Nigeria were circumscribed due to the Christiano–Fitzgerald (CF) filter; hence, analysis was limited until 2009. Least efficiency is seen in 1998–2001, a booming phase, which would go against economic intuition except researchers found Nigerian investors to be more interested in short-term gains and chose to ignore long-term investment opportunities (see Olweni, 2011). This also explains the higher level of efficiency in short term for the same time period.

Table 5.12 Business cycles and efficiency for the UAE

		Efficiency	
		Short term	*Long term*
1998M07–1999M07	Boom	0.3174	0.2487
1999M08–2000M10	**Recession**	**0.2427**	**0.2013**
2000M11–2002M04	Boom	0.2013	0.1051
2002M05–2003M05	**Recession**	**0.3180**	**0.1288**
2003M06–2004M02	Boom	0.2252	0.0912
2004M03–2005M03	**Recession**	**0.1210**	**0.1416**
2005M04–2007M02	Boom	0.2604	0.2014
2007M03–2008M03	**Recession**	**0.2130**	**0.2516**
2008M04–2009M08	Boom	0.0351	0.3626
2009M09–2014M12	**Recession**	**0.1593**	**0.1094**

Table 5.13 Business cycles and efficiency for Nigeria

		Efficiency	
		Short term	*Long term*
1996M03–1997M02	Boom	0.2895	0.1612
1998M01–1998M11	**Recession**	**0.1076**	**0.2678**
1998M12–2001M09	Boom	0.1323	0.4749
2001M10–2005M01	**Recession**	**0.2486**	**0.0997**
2005M02–2006M11	Boom	0.1803	0.3771
2006M12–2009M03	**Recession**	**0.3805**	**0.3285**

The Nigerian economy further soared in the early 2000s in response to higher oil prices, as seen in the higher efficiency levels during the long term for 2001–2005. This was further exacerbated by the approval, by the Paris Club, of a debt-relief deal to eliminate US$ 18 billion in debt for US$ 12 billion in payment and Nigeria was able to pay off its debt by 2006.

Saudi Arabia

From Table 5.14, higher inefficiency is seen in 1998–1999, which was when the Saudi Arabian economy was affected by the low oil prices in 1997, and increase in oil production by non-OPEC countries, the stock market was at its peak of inefficiency for both short-term and long-term periods.

Table 5.14 Business cycles and efficiency for Saudi Arabia

		Efficiency	
		Short term	*Long term*
1998M02–1999M07	**Recession**	**0.2421**	**0.3171**
1999M08–2000M11	Boom	0.2024	0.2344
2000M12–2002M03	**Recession**	**0.1945**	**0.2066**
2002M04–2003M04	Boom	0.0931	0.3541
2003M05 2004M01	**Recession**	**0.1565**	**0.3010**
2004M02–2005M02	Boom	0.1714	0.5930
2005M03–2007M05	**Recession**	**0.0529**	**0.1718**
2007M06–2008M05	Boom	0.1591	0.0369
2008M06–2009M07	**Recession**	**0.2399**	**0.1776**
2009M08–2012M03	Boom	0.1556	0.1727
2012M04–2014M12	**Recession**	**0.2076**	**0.1756**

In an event known as Riyadh's Black Monday, the Tadawul plunged 20% in 2006 causing the market to collapse. The volatility mainly bubbled from too much money being invested. As the country was enjoying its oil money, domestic investors chose to invest their money in the stock market causing it to become a bubble, which eventually burst. This had increased the volatility of the stock market but not the efficiency. The stock market remained efficient during this period.

Table 5.15 Business cycles and efficiency for Qatar

		Efficiency	
		Short term	*Long term*
1998M02–1999M08	**Recession**	**1.0611**	**0.3374**
1999M09–2000M11	Boom	0.5415	0.4701
2000M12–2002M03	**Recession**	**0.3411**	**0.3959**
2002M04–2003M07	Boom	0.2385	0.383
2003M08–2004M07	**Recession**	**0.2907**	**0.3777**
2004M08–2005M08	Boom	0.3036	0.5611
2005M09–2007M03	**Recession**	**0.8858**	**0.3580**
2007M04–2008M04	Boom	0.3359	0.1461
2008M05–2009M07	**Recession**	**0.1767**	**0.4297**
2009M08–2011M11	Boom	0.2290	0.1286
2011M12–2014M12	**Recession**	**0.0793**	**0.1103**

Qatar

An anomaly of efficiency higher than 1.0 is rejected from the analysis. Therefore, Qatar least efficient period was the 2005–2007 recession for the short term (See Table 5.15). Qatar established major liberalization in its financial market in 2005. The liberalization included removing restriction on foreign participation in the market. However, during this period, the market was recorded to be inefficient. This goes against previous studies that argue that financial liberalization have positive impact on the efficiency of a market.

5.7 Conclusion

Analysing the efficiency of markets provides vital insight for the regulators and global investors and has implications for investment strategies and theory for the academic literature. The current literature is rife with evidential proof on the linkage between stock markets and economic state, with stock markets trumping as the lead indicator for the economy of the country. This chapter attempts to analyse the market efficiency of OIC member countries, differing from other efficiency studies by incorporating the element of business cycles. Furthermore, the efficiency of the markets in relation to the different phases of the business cycle is measured.

This analysis contributes towards the literature through an empirical analysis of the stock markets links with efficiency in the OIC. It tests the weak form efficiency on 11 major OIC member countries and determines the degree of efficiency while accounting for the different economic phases impelling the country.

The analysis reveals, overall the countries show a trend of improving efficiency throughout the sample period. Furthermore, while the results concur with previous research on the economic intuition that efficiency is better during economic booms than during bust, there are several instances when the data does not reflect this. However, most of these instances can be explained by economic, political or other concurring situations that may have affected the stock market.

Note

1. See Pasquini and Serva (1999), Kwapien et al. (2005) and Oswiecimka et al. (2005)

References

Blume, L., & Durlauf, S. (2007). *The new Palgrave: A dictionary of economics*, Second Edition. New York: Palgrave Macmillan.

Cajueiro, D. O., Gogas, P., & Tabak, B. M. (2009). Does financial market liberalization increase the degree of market efficiency? The case of the Athens stock exchange. *International Review of Financial Analysis*, *18*(1), 50–57.

Fama, E. (1990). Term-structure forecast of interest rates, inflation, and real returns. *Journal of Monetary Economics*, *25*(1), 59–76.

Fama, E. F. (1965). The behaviour of stock-market prices. *The Journal of Business*, *38*(1), 34–105.

Jensen, M. C. (1978). Some anomalous evidence regarding market efficiency. *Journal of Financial Economics*, *6*(1), 95–101.

Kantelhardt, J. W., Zschiengerm, S. A., Koscienly-Bunde, E., Havlin, S., Bunde, A., & Stanley, H. E. (2002). Multifractal detrended fluctuation analysis of nonstationary time series. *Physica A*, *316*, 87–114.

Kwapien, J., Oswie, P. C., & Drozdz, S. (2005). Components of multifractality in high-frequency stock returns. *Physica A*, *350*(2–4), 466–474.

Malkiel, B. (1992). Ef ficient market hypothesis. In P. Newman, M. Milgate, & J. Eatwell (Eds.), *New Palgrave dictionary of money and finance*. London: Macmillan.

Olweny, T. (2011). Modelling Volatility of Short-term Interest Rates in Kenya. *International Journal of Business and Social Science*, *2*(7), 289–303.

Oswiecimkaa, P., Kwapien, J., Celinska, I., Drozdza, S., & Rak, R. (2005). Multifractality in the stock market: Price increments versus waiting times. *Physica A*, *347*, 626–638.

Pasquini, M., & Serva, M. (1999). Clustering of volatility as a multiscale phenomenon. *European Physical Journal B: Condensed Matter and Complex Systems*, *16*(1), 195–201.

Peng, C. K., Buldyrev, S. V., Havlin, S., M., Stanley, H. E., & Coldberger, A. L. (1994). Mosaic organization of DNA nucleotides. *Physical Review E*, *49*, 1685–1689.

Pesaran, M. H. (2005). Market efficiency today (Working Paper 05.41). Resource document. Institute of Economic Policy Research. http://www.usc.edu/dept/LAS/economics/IEPR/Working%20Papers/IEPR_05.41_%5BPesaran%5D.pdf. Accessed 12 June 2016.

Rizvi, S. A. R., Dewandaru, G., Bacha, O., & Masih, M. (2014). An analysis of stock market efficiency: developed vs Islamic stock markets using MF-DFA. *Physica A*, *407*, 86–99.

Samuelson, P. A. (1965). Proof that properly anticipated prices fluctuate randomly. *Industrial Management Review*, *6*(2), 1–9.

CHAPTER 6

Investigating the Integration

Abstract Analysing the market integration is an important part of understanding the economic nature of a stock market as it tells us its relationship with world markets and its effect based on movements in other markets. Organization of Islamic Cooperation (OIC) member countries, with higher volatility and greater market instability, are of particular interest in understanding how their markets would react to global or regional news. This chapter will analyse comparatively with developed markets the market integration of OIC member countries with the world average as well look into its regional integration.

Keywords Market integration · Regional integration · ICAPM · Market reaction

6.1 Introduction

Financial market integration is the process of uniting markets to allow for cross-border capital flows without many obstructions (Frijins et al. 2012). Usually, trade and investment barriers are lifted or reduced, communication and transportation linkages improved, and by forming economic or political unions (such as the European Union or the Organization of Islamic Cooperation (OIC)). Many countries opt for market integration as it offers several benefits such as portfolio diversification leading to

S. Arshad, *Stock Markets in Islamic Countries*, Palgrave CIBFR Studies in Islamic Finance, DOI 10.1007/978-3-319-47803-6_6

reduced risks, financial stability by allowing efficient allocation of capital and enhancing competition among financial intermediaries.

When markets are fully integrated, similar risk profile assets should have the same price even if they are traded on different markets. Investors face common and country-specific or idiosyncratic risk, but the price of the asset in a fully integrated market only reflects common risk factors, as idiosyncratic risks are fully diversifiable. In a partially integrated market, the asset price will reflect both the common risk and country specific risks, whereas, in a completely segmented market, the price would only reflect the country specific source of risk. Hence, the same asset can have different returns owing to the different risk profile based on the integration of its market.

Hence, considering this, this chapter examines comparatively the extent of underdevelopment of stock markets in the OIC vis-à-vis more developed stock markets and measures the level of integration with the world for both groups of countries. Employing the International Capital Asset Pricing Model (ICAPM), this chapter strives to find the level of integration amongst the markets selected.

6.2 Why Study Market Integration?

Robson (1980) defines integration as a state of affair or a process that involves any attempt to combine separate national economies into larger economic regions. Integration could be beneficial as it increases trade or improve the division of labour amongst countries, giving rise to specialized labour.

When studying the integration of capital markets, the term 'market integration' in the literature represents a rather broad area of research; however, it can be narrowed down based on asset pricing or statistical perspective. The studies on perfectly integrated markets based on asset pricings often are defined by their observation of the 'law of one price'. This observation branches from the logical implication that if two or more markets are integrated then indistinguishable securities should be priced identically as they would have the same risk characteristics regardless of the country of origin. Whereas, the statistical approach suggests that if prices in the national stock markets share a long-term equilibrium relationship, the markets are said to be integrated. This chapter adopts the asset pricing view in measuring stock market integration amongst OIC member countries.

Emerging markets, over the past decade, have gone through a myriad of changes, from economic reforms to financial liberalization. An important agenda in all of this was to allow for a well-developed stock market, which could boast lower cost of capital, higher savings, growth and investments opportunities. However, it is also within the same period, that a sequence of severe crises affected and altered permanently the exposure of national markets to global risk factors as well as their degree of integration. Yet, most of today's markets are neither perfectly integrated nor strictly segmented.

Moreover, financial integration also influences the volatility of business cycles, as integration among international markets intensifies the effects of existing distortions plaguing national financial markets. Over the past decades, cross-border financial integration has increased significantly, where around the same time as business cycles started synchronizing. Furthermore, in the wake of the largest economic crisis since the great depression, many argue that financial linkages acted as a facilitator for its transmission.

Therefore, it becomes vital to study how international financial market integration contributes towards business cycle volatility. International business cycle theories suggest that in the absence of major financial shocks, integration of financial markets should amplify the effect of total factor productivity shocks and thus cause output patterns to diverge.

6.3 Market Integration in the Oic

The documentation of stock market integration among OIC countries and its relationship with other markets is significantly inadequate with most of the research focusing on the markets either individually or regionally.

Some research indicated that the OIC stock markets are segmented regionally but integrated internationally and that cointegration strengthened after the September 11, incident. Neaime (2002) studied the Gulf Cooperation Council (GCC) and Middle East–North Africa (MENA) equity markets and found Turkey, Egypt, Morocco and Jordanian market to be integrated with world financial markets. Other researchers (see Hassan and Javed 2010) found Karachi stock market to not cointegrated with other emerging markets within the OIC. Similarly, the Turkish stock market was integrated with Indonesian and Egyptian markets.

A few studies have attempted to measure the level of stock market integration in the case of Turkey, and found contrasting results. Gokcen and Ozturkmen (1997) found that Istanbul stock market is segmented from developed market during the period of 1989–1993.

6.4 Relationship Between Business Cycles and Market Integration

When reviewing the degree of financial integration in general, there is vast research available on developed countries, focusing mainly on the major markets globally. Another popular trend in the literature is a comparison amongst the major markets or between developed and developing markets.

The degree of integration differs over different segments considerably. The banking markets, for instance, was found to converge across Europe towards interest rate, whereas, retail interest rates showed a relatively high degree of dispersion across countries.[1] Similarly, the interbank and the corporate bond market in Europe showed higher levels of integration, whereas collaterized money markets and equity markets are nation specific.

Through market integration, economies become more proficient in absorbing shocks and are able to foster regional development. One indication of this is the Asian crisis of 1997–1998 where economists argued that one of the main contributors to the crisis was the lack of a strongly integrated regional financial market.

The study of financial market integration along with the comovements of business cycles across countries has received little attention in the literature. Some found that financial integration had a positive effect on cyclical comovements.[2] On the link between volatility and integration, the empirical literature suggests that the degree of interdependence of markets is higher during periods of crisis as opposed to periods of growth. This can be explained by the 'overreaction' of investors to bad news. Furthermore, globalization has brought about structural changes in the global financial system in the long term while having short-term impact on the development of the financial environment, which in turn intensifies the contagion between equity markets.

While much of the empirical evidences suggest that cross-border financial integration leads to greater international transmission and greater business cycle comovements, it goes against the international real business cycle models. Proponents of the model found that an increase in cross-border financial integration lead to a fall in business cycle correlation across countries.

6.5 Theory Behind Market Integration

The approach taken to measure the degree of integration between markets finds its roots in the Capital Asset Pricing Model (CAPM). The CAPM pioneered by Sharpe (1964) and Lintner (1965) changed the course of finance, as it offers a powerful and intuitive prediction on measuring risk and the relationship between expected return and risk. However, one setback of this widely used model is its lack of empirical record owing mainly to its many simplifying assumptions or the inability to test the model (Fama and French 2004).

The CAPM enlists the use of beta for pricing stocks to determine its cost if capital which will allow for a reasonable estimate of market integration. One assumption of the CAPM model is that if there is equilibrium in the market than expected returns represent fair compensation for the degree of risk each security contributes towards a portfolio.

Bodnar et al. (2003), on the other hand, defines global market integration as a function of the portfolio choices of a company's stockholders. Integration is likely to occur when a company's stockholder holds globally diversified portfolios. Reversely, when a company's stockholders are located and invest in home country, it calls for segmentation.

The ICAPM of Solnik, (1974), Stulz, (1981) and Adler and Dumas (1983), stems from the violation of the purchasing power parity (PPP) in the long and short run, where the asset might yield different returns for different investors in different countries. As investors also bear exchange risk along with market risk. The foreign exchange risk is just the percentage difference between forward and spot rate due to the deviations of the PPP.

Furthermore, empirical tests on the ICAPM have so far been inconclusive, falling into three broad categories. First, it is considered an international version of the basic CAPM developed by Sharpe and Linter.[3] Second, some literature is found to test the unconditional version of the ICAPM as developed by Solnik, (1974), Stulz, (1981) and Adler and Dumas (1983). This group concludes that both the CAPM and ICAPM provide indistinguishable results, in application to individual firms. Lastly, the third category focuses on a conditional version of the ICAPM based on the condition that investors base their portfolio allocations on presently available information.[4]

Hence, in the absence of an established theoretical model that postulates the mechanisms moving a market from segmentation to integrated, this essay employs the ICAPM model to gauge the integration level of OIC member countries. This analysis relies on the work of Pukthuanthong and Roll (2009) that developed a principal component regression in which an index's return is regressed on 10 global factors. The R^2 from their regression captured the degree of market integration, consequently providing evidence of market integration. They found that emerging markets remained partially segmented while developed markets were highly integrated with the world market.

6.6 Data Selection

This research consists of 10 OIC member countries, selected based on the top 20 exchanges of the world by market capitalization and hinged on the availability of data, as discussed in Chapter 4. The developed markets are also selected based on market capitalization as an indicator of market development, which ultimately represent the measure of size and liquidity.

The US market is not included, as the global index is heavily constituted of US-based companies, which may provide biased results for the measure of integration. Moreover, the level of integration results could be fouled due to the near standstill of capital markets in the USA during the sub-prime crisis.

Monthly share prices of constituent companies of all 13 countries in the sample obtained are from DataStream and the sample period ranges from 1999 to 2014. Table 6.1 details the countries selected in the sample:

Table 6.1 List of countries selected

Islamic countries	*Developed countries*
Bangladesh	United Kingdom
Egypt	France
Indonesia	Germany
Jordan	
Kuwait	
Malaysia	
Oman	
Pakistan	
Saudi Arabia	
Turkey	

Table 6.2 Number of listed companies from the S&P BMI

Country	*No. of listed companies*
Bangladesh	373
Egypt	535
Indonesia	867
Jordan	273
Kuwait	251
Malaysia	949
Oman	160
Pakistan	532
Saudi Arabia	169
Turkey	670
UK	846
France	735
Germany	604

The market indices obtained are from the Standard & Poor Broad Market Index (S&P BMI) rather than individual market index to maintain homogeneity in data source. As different index have different ways of calculating indices, the use of S&P BMI will reduce the risk of dissimilarity in indices. Table 6.2 details the number of companies selected for each country.

6.7 Methodology

Below a brief description of the methodologies used to find market integration are presented:

6.7.1 International Capital Asset Pricing Model (ICAPM)

This study relies on the ICAPM model to learn about the level of market integration. Bruner et al. (2008) employed a cost of capital comparative analysis implied by the local and international CAPM as a proxy for market integration.

This proxy is further encouraged from the empirical works of Koedikij et al. (2002), where it was found that there was almost same costs of equity capital between local and international CAPM, with or without adjusting for exchange rates. Thus, Bruner contended that if the fit between local and international beta were better, the level of market integration of the country with world would be higher. Following the work of Bruner et al. (2008) and Pukthuanthong and Roll (2009), the current research will shadow a similar method of determining integration.

There are several advantages of this method over other alternatives:

1. ICAPM treats the dynamic process of market integration as opposed to a static one.
2. Estimating the integration over the cross-section of stock returns can effectively deal with structural breaks whereas a time series-based method would require additional handling.
3. The results are less biased towards large-cap stocks as it uses whole cross-section of stocks within a country.

For each country, first estimate the local or domestic CAPM by running a regression of each company's monthly excess return on its respective local market index over a rolling window of 36 months as follows:

$$r_{it} - r_{ft} = \alpha_{it}^{C} + \beta_{it}^{C}(r_{Ct} - r_{ft}) + \varepsilon_{it}, \tag{6.1}$$

where r_{it} is the US dollar return on stock i, r_{Ct} is the US dollar return on the local market index (this essay uses the S&P BMI), r_{ft} is the risk-free rate proxied by the 3-month US Treasury Bill and β_{it}^{C} is the market beta of stock i on the local index for window τ. The US Treasury Bill is used as the risk-free rate to allow for a smoother transition of analysis. Owing to the limited nature of data on developing countries, procuring the risk-free rate for each sample country was not possible. Furthermore, this research draws its motivation in applying the US Treasury Bill as the risk-free rate from several other researches.[5] These researchers have used 3-month US Treasury Bills or 1-month euro dollar deposit rate as a proxy for the risk-free rate when analysing the market integration of developing countries.

To obtain beta of each company within a country, this regression is rolled on a monthly basis. Similarly, we run regressions on a global market index (the S&B World Broad Market Index) over a rolling window of 36 months as follows:

$$r_{it} - r_{ft} = \alpha_{it}^{W} + \beta_{it}^{W}(r_{wt} - r_{ft}) + n_{it}, \tag{6.2}$$

where r_{wt} is the US dollar return on the global market index and β_{it}^{W} is the beta on the global market index for stock i for window.

Merging the estimations of Eqs. 6.1 and 6.2 gives a panel of beta coefficients for local and global CAPM. Subsequently, using Bruner et al. (2008) as a guide, we estimate the cross-sectional regressions of the global beta on the domestic beta for all companies in each country to measure for the degree of integration with the world, as shown below:

$$\beta_{it}^{W} = \gamma_{0\tau} + \gamma_{1\tau}\beta_{it}^{C} + \zeta_{i\tau}. \tag{6.3}$$

The measure of integration will be obtained from the R^2 value of this regression. Estimating the above equation per country on a cross-sectional basis for each window of τ, obtains a time series of R^2 for each country. Hence, the higher the R^2, the better the fit between domestic and global market beta, that is, there is a higher level of integration. Meanwhile, a lower R^2 indicates that the two betas generated different estimates on the cost of capital, signifying segmented markets.

6.7.2 *Multivariate GARCH*

Multivariate General Autoregressive Conditional Hetrosckedascity (MGARCH) is used to derive the regional conditional volatility and volatility interdependence of the stock market and business cycles for sample countries. First modelled by Bollerslev et al. (1988), the MGARCH model allows the conditional covariance matrix of the dependent variables to follow a flexible dynamic structure and further allows the conditional mean to follow a vector autoregressive assembly.

In general, the MGARCH model can be written as:

$$y_t = Cx_t + \varepsilon_t, \tag{6.4}$$

$$\varepsilon_t = H_t^{1/2} + \nu_t, \tag{6.5}$$

where y_t is the m-vector of dependent variables, C is a m x k parameter matrix. x_t is defined as the k-vector of explanatory variables inclusive of y_t lags. $H_t^{1/2}$ is the Cholesky factor of the time-varying conditional covariance matrix H_t. Lastly, v_t is an m-vector of zero mean, unit variance i.i.d. innovations.

6.8 Analysis and Results

To begin, the business cycle obtained through the Christiano–Fitzgerald filter are as follows:

From Fig. 6.1, the various business cycle turns in each sample country is seen. A palpable observation is that the business cycle curves for the developed countries are much smoother than the OIC member countries. This is because most of the OIC member countries are developing or emerging markets hence are more susceptible to recessions, whereas developed countries, with developed financial and economic structures are able to weather smaller variances to their economy. Another commonalty in the graphs above is the impact of the global financial crisis. All 13 countries felt the effect of the crisis, signalling great interdependence and a contagion effect amongst the countries and with the USA.

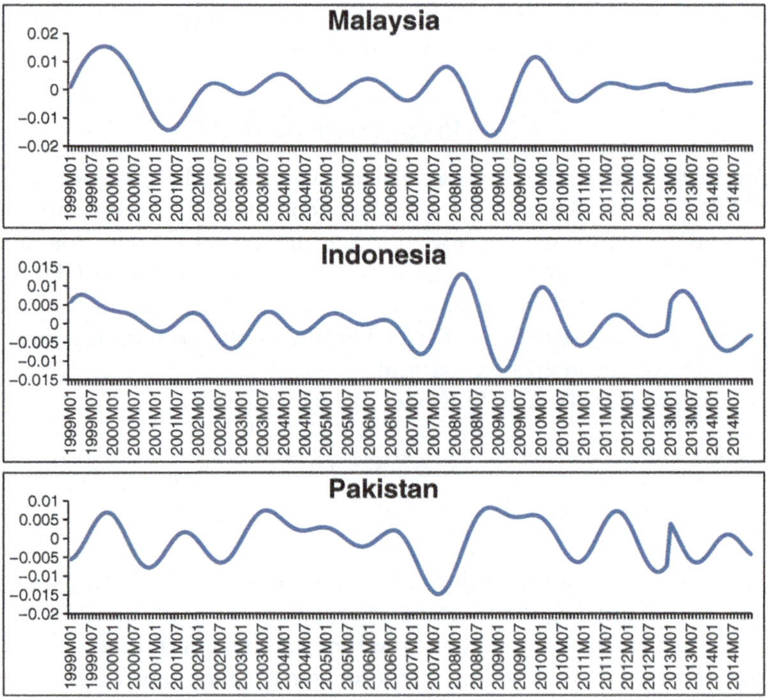

Fig. 6.1 Business cycle graphs for each sample country

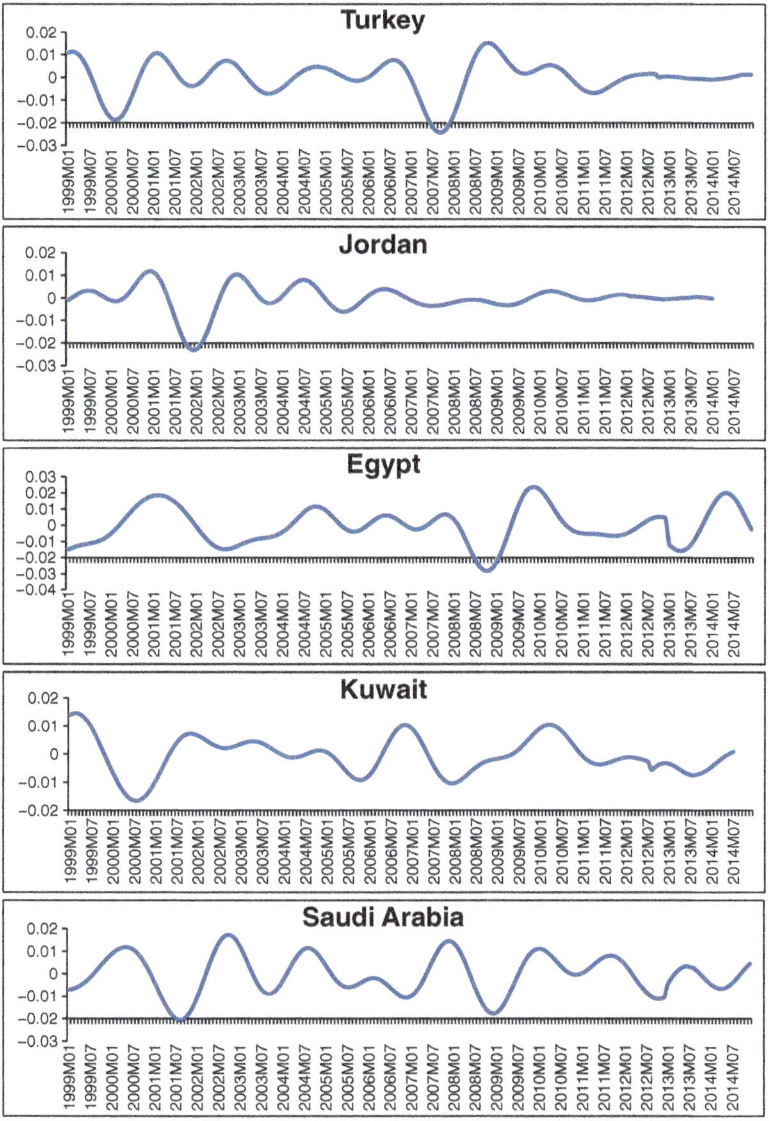

Fig. 6.1 continued

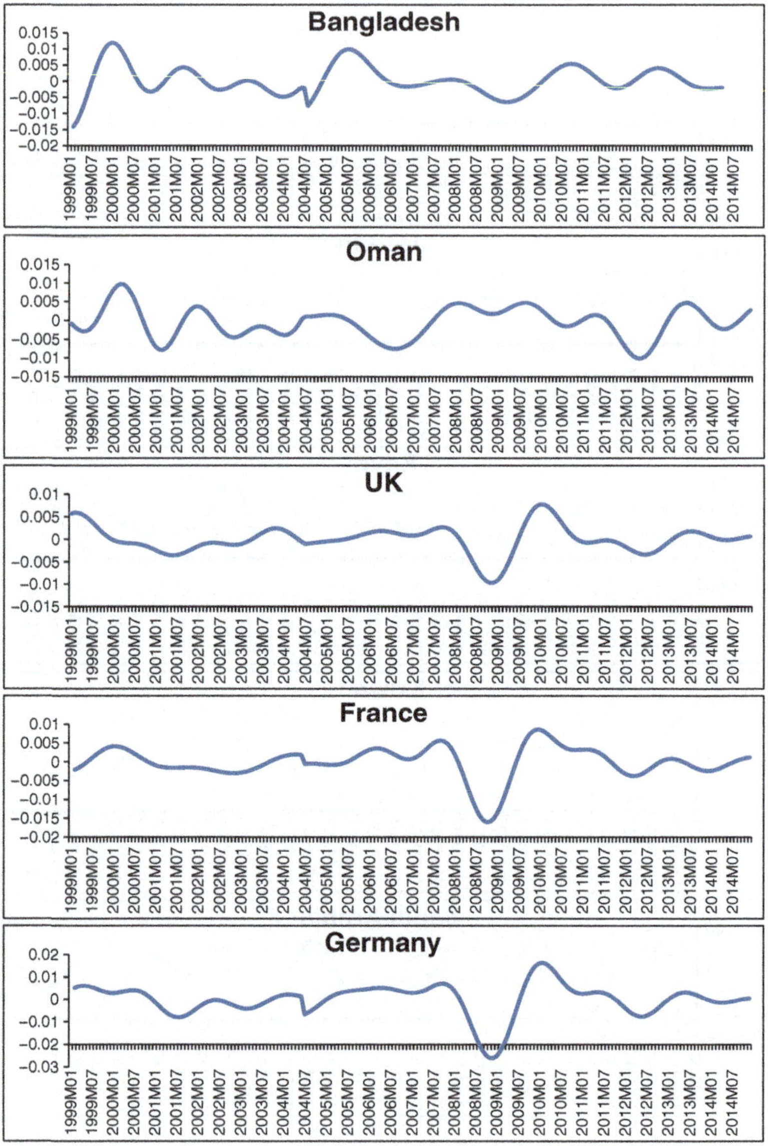

Fig. 6.1 continued

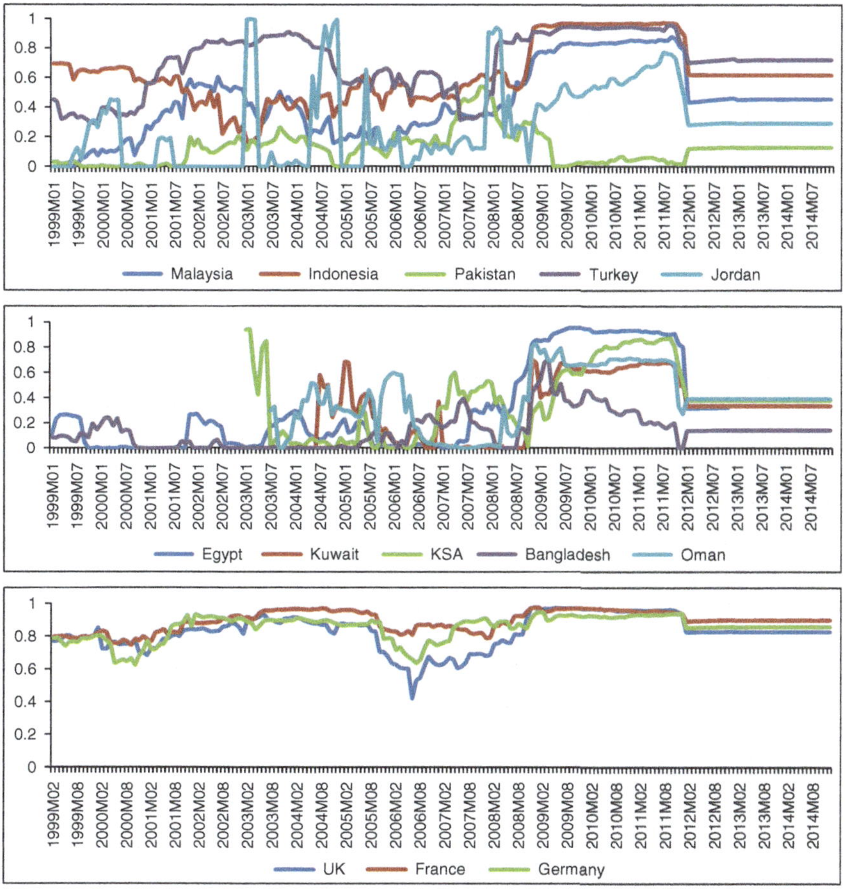

Fig. 6.2 FMarket integration with world benchmark for sample countries

Within the framework of International CAPM, this analysis strives to study the level of integration for a sample of 10 OIC member countries and three developed markets to allow for a comparative evaluation. The graphs in Fig. 6.2 depict the 36-month rolling windows of estimated R^2 between global and domestic betas for each individual country for the sample period of 1999–2014.

From the Islamic countries, Malaysia, Indonesia and Turkey follow a relatively more stable pattern of integration, which is in line with its comparatively higher stage of market development amongst the OIC countries. Bangladesh has the lowest level of market integration amongst sample countries. Interestingly, in the aftermath of the global crisis, it is seen that all countries converged towards the world index, with the exception of Pakistan and Bangladesh. On the other hand, the developed countries have maintained their level of integration throughout the sample period with little deviations from the world index.

6.8.1 Country-wise Analysis

Below each country is investigated separately in accordance to their business cycles to understand the effect different phases of business cycle have on the market integration. The level of integration is understood that as it approaches one it means it is fully integrated with the world index.

Malaysia

From Table 6.3, a weak integration level for Malaysia can be seen for the year 1999, which is attributed to the austere capital controls consequent to the 1-year ban of removing portfolio capital for foreign investors in 1998. These capital control measures contributed to the recovery of the Malaysian stock market, whereby many foreign portfolio investors became more interested in investing there.

From the point of view of the investors, Malaysia had offered a relatively sheltered portfolio from global volatility. In 1999, it was replaced by a

Table 6.3 Business cycles and integration: Malaysia

		Average growth	*Integration*
Growth	1999M01–2000M08	1.048%	0.0741
Recession	**2000M09–2002M01**	**–0.852%**	**0.3736**
Growth	2002M02–2004M06	0.206%	0.4345
Recession	**2004M07–2005M6**	**–0.267%**	**0.2222**
Growth	2005M07–2006M06	0.270%	0.2122
Recession	**2006M07–2007M03**	**–0.248%**	**0.3251**
Growth	2007M04–2008M03	0.520%	0.3571
Recession	**2008M04–2009M05**	**–1.004%**	**0.6365**
Growth	2009M06–2010M06	0.735%	0.8301
Recession	**2010M07–2011M03**	**–0.262%**	**0.8447**
Growth	2011M04–2014M12	0.158%	**0.6167**

graduated tax on outflows, allowing the Malaysian market to be more integrated. Unfortunately, this integration only lasted until 2002, after which market integration level started to fall again.

In 2003, Malaysia sought to remove all outflow restrictions, which unfortunately only had an ephemeral response and market integration levels remained low until 2005. This long period of underwhelming market integration suggests the long-term impact of capital control for Malaysian equity market. The Malaysian economy had remained favourable to foreign investors as foreign direct investments (FDIs) grew from RM 129.1 billion in 2001 to RM 253.8 billion in 2007. Investors had confidence in the Malaysian market, which is why the relinquishment of the fixed exchange rate regime in July 2005 did not have significant impact on the market integration.

Owing to its emerging nature, Malaysia was significantly affected by the global crisis of 2008, as can be seen through its business cycle, where a significant decline in Industrial Production is witnessed. The crisis of 2008 had a more severe impact on Malaysia than the Asian crisis of 1997 as the Malaysian market was more segmented from the world market in the 1990s. As the Malaysian market grew more integrated, the impact from any external shock was felt significantly.

In regards to the link between business cycle and integration, literature shows that market integration tends to be higher during recessionary periods, which is only reflective in the last two recessions Malaysia faced, owing to the global nature of the recession. Measuring market integration with the world, Malaysia is seen not to have high integration during the Asian financial crisis of 1997, as Malaysia's reach was regional as opposed to later years, when Malaysia started opening its market to foreign investors. This is reflected in the global financial crisis of 2008, where Malaysia is highly integrated.

Indonesia

The Indonesian market is in contrast to the Malaysian market, where reliance on the International Monetary Fund (IMF) allowed Indonesia to avoid any penalty on the market. It is seen that the Indonesian market remained steady after the Asian crisis. The Indonesian market felt a significant impact in the following years of 2001–2002 where a series of ill-fated events shattered the confidence of investors. The market was blemished with global impacts of the World Trade

Table 6.4 Business cycles and integration: Indonesia

		Average growth	*Integration*
Growth	1999M01–2000M10	0.448%	0.6507
Recession	**2000M11–2003M04**	**-0.144%**	**0.4176**
Growth	2003M05–2006M07	0.081%	0.4712
Recession	**2006M08–2007M08**	**-0.465%**	**0.5016**
Growth	2007M09–2008M08	0.851%	0.5900
Recession	**2008M09–2009M08**	**-0.757%**	**0.9381**
Growth	2009M09–2010M07	0.638%	0.9627
Recession	**2010M08–2014M12**	**-0.002%**	**0.8113**

Centre terrorist attacks, dotcom crisis, collapse of Enron and perhaps more importantly the Bali bombings.

A sharp increase in the degree of integration began in 2003, as in Table 6.4 is explained by Indonesia's openness to foreign trade, high growth rates and effects of international financial shocks. Overall, Indonesia appears to be less integrated than the other Asian OIC members mainly due to:

1. Its underdeveloped and small domestic capital markets;
2. The heterogeneous nature of the region and the difference in size between the other countries;
3. Its regulatory practices that tend to discriminate ex post against the cross-border activity of Asian banks;
4. Capital account restrictions that limit the scope for two-way capital flows.

Once again, in 2006, the Indonesian economy was plunged into recession in the reverberation of the December 2004 tsunami. In 2005, the economy was able to stay afloat despite crumpling real wages, high inflation, rising unemployment and contracting consumer credit. However, the effects of which reared its ugly head in 2006 resulting in a credit crunch. While the economy had declined significantly, the market integration level remained constant through this only to fall again during the global financial crisis.

Interestingly, the drop in integration did not occur during the recession period, but rather before the economy took a downfall. The Indonesian market, in the aftermath of the global crisis became highly integrated with the world index.

Pakistan

The Pakistani market, on the other hand, began the oldest stock market amongst the OIC member countries, placed capital controls owing to economic embargos in 1998 post-May 1998 nuclear test. This is reflected in its weak integration with the world through the major first half of the period, as seen in Table 6.5.

In 2002, Pakistan was reported to be the best performing market in the world, which continued over the next 3 years, reflected in improved macroeconomic conditions, low interest rates and excess liquidity. Furthermore, regulatory improvements and a revival of the economy post-2005 increased the foreign portfolio investments, mirrored in the increasing levels of market integration. However, this resurgence did not last long, as another set of capital controls on stock markets were put in place in 2008 owing to a 60% decline in the benchmark index.

Turkey

Turkey's political turmoil, in particular its significant budget deficit in 1999, instigated weak integration levels in the earlier periods of the study, seen in Table 6.6. The integration levels recovered 2003 onwards when Turkey structurally reformed its foreign investment regulations. Turkey had been absorbing substantial amounts of foreign inflows since its gradual liberalization in 1980s, these reforms boosted the confidence post-crisis.

Integration levels rose in 2003 in line with the crisis and began to decline in 2005 illustrating erratic behaviours until 2007. The global crisis of 2007–2008 impacted the Turkish economy and also dropped the integration level significantly owing to dropping oil prices and global

Table 6.5 Business cycles and integration: Pakistan

		Average growth	*Integration*
Growth	1999M06–2000M05	0.439%	0.0040
Recession	**2000M06–2002M12**	**-0.332%**	**0.0753**
Growth	2003M01–2005M06	0.370%	0.1399
Recession	**2005M07–2008M03**	**-0.444%**	**0.2646**
Growth	2008M04–2010M05	0.579%	0.1094
Recession	**2010M06–2011M04**	**-0.386%**	**0.0512**
Growth	2011M05–2012M03	0.476%	0.0556
Recession	**2012M04–2014M12**	**-0.644%**	**0.1268**

Table 6.6 Business cycles and integration: Turkey

		Average growth	*Integration*
Growth	1999M01 -1999M07	0.856%	0.3686
Recession	**1999M08–2000M08**	**-1.257%**	**0.3479**
Growth	2000M09–2003M03	0.394%	0.7254
Recession	**2003M04–2004M03**	**-0.456%**	**0.8815**
Growth	2004M04–2006M12	0.322%	0.6360
Recession	**2007M01–2008M04**	**-1.43%**	**0.4939**
Growth	2008M05–2010M09	0.68%	0.9141
Recession	**2010M10–2014M12**	**-0.379%**	**0.9203**

crashes of stock markets and economies alike. The integration level shot up again post-crisis.

Bangladesh

The market integration data for Bangladesh is sporadic owing to insufficient data available. Nonetheless, the level of market integration has remained low throughout the sample period mainly attributed to economic and political instability and underdevelopment of its stock market.

Since the early 1990, the Bangladesh economy had undergone a steady restructuring of the industrial sector to strengthen the fiscal and monetary management. This led to macroeconomic stability and a positive impact on the country's ability to attract FDIs, thus leading to an increase in market integration in 2000. However, this did not last long, as in 2001 a confluence of external factors, extending from a recession and the September 11 attacks, the economy declined and Bangladesh was subject to discriminatory trade and investment practices.

The results represented in Table 6.7, suggest that the impact of the crisis on the Bangladesh economy has been mild with a modest slowdown in the economy, while having devastating effects on the equity markets. With some comovements with the US economy, the crisis of 2007 also affected the Bangladesh economy. Furthermore, market integration also increased significantly at this point.

Egypt

Throughout the sample period, Egypt has shown low levels of market integration as seen in Table 6.8. This is related to the emerging nature of

Table 6.7 Business Cycles and Integration: Bangladesh

		Average growth	*Integration*
Recession	**1999M01–1999M07**	**-0.792%**	**0.0859**
Growth	1998M08–2000M08	0.764%	0.1602
Recession	**2000M09–2001M03**	**-0.022%**	**0.0252**
Growth	2001M04–2002M02	0.284%	0.0140
Recession	**2002M03–2004M08**	**-0.189%**	**0.0051**
Growth	2004M09–2006M07	0.149%	0.0567
Recession	**2006M08–2007M07**	**-0.280%**	**0.2409**
Growth	2007M08–2008M09	0.418%	0.1119

Table 6.8 Business cycles and integration: Egypt

		Average growth	*Integration*
Recession	**1999M01–2000M03**	**-0.909%**	**0.13008**
Growth	2000M04–2001M12	1.269%	0.02737
Recession	**2002M01–2004M02**	**-0.874%**	**0.14521**
Growth	2004M03–2008M02	0.364%	0.10747
Recession	**2008M03–2009M04**	**-1.759%**	**0.61754**
Growth	2009M05–2010M08	1.42%	0.93796
Recession	**2010M09–2014M04**	**-0.46%**	**0.91068**

the economy and the underdevelopment of the financial market. During the recession periods, of 2000–2001 and 2004–2008, the level of integration has remained significantly lower than in periods of boom, owing to a drop in share prices. In the first quarter of 2000, a surge of consolidations took place in the cement and banking sectors driving up share prices.

With liquidity tied up in the cement shares, the market began to fall, resulting in decreased integration. The decline in the market continued until 2001 attributable to the global downturn, slow speed of privatization and political circumstances in the Middle East region. This period shows a clear departure from the semi-strong efficient market hypothesis with two specific characteristics of first, leakage of information prior to announcement date and second, a slow readjustment following the announcement dates of the consolidations.

Integration levels dropped once again in 2003 attributed mainly to the tightening of the lending criteria following the passing of the Money Laundry Law 80 in 2002 and the Banking Law in 2003. Since interest rates were no longer the dominating factor in bank lending decisions, coupled with inefficient supervision of the central bank, it led to the non-performing loan crisis. This is also responsible for the low levels of integration during that period. Nevertheless, integration did rise after 2003 because of the agreement between Egypt, Jordan and Syria to extend its liquefied natural gas pipeline, which also allowed the economy to recover.

Another factor responsible for the weak integration level in 2003 is the Iraq war. The Iraq war had a strop impact on the Egyptian market, where many investors suffered substantial losses and low returns. In this analysis, beta for the market for this period to be 0.127% on average, hence the impact of the Iraq war is higher on the beta of Egypt and Morocco as compared to other countries in the region.

The only incongruity to the above is during the recession post-crisis in mid-2008, where integration levels have rapidly been increasing to become highly integrated with world index consequently from a contagion effect of the crisis.

Jordan

Despite being one of the most open to foreign investors and most sophisticated among Arab countries (Gentzoglanis 2007), the Jordanian market shows low levels of integration with world index, which can be seen in Table 6.9. Particularly for the period of 2001 and 2002 which was also a recession period for Jordan. Owing to the September 11 attacks on the USA, the market integration dropped tremendously. Intriguingly, the market integration shot up in 2003 facing the Iraq war.

During the boom periods of end-2002 onwards, the stock market also experienced boom in accordance with an increase in foreign inflows. The

Table 6.9 Business cycles and integration: Jordan

		Average growth	*Integration*
Growth	1999M02–2001M05	0.408%	0.136301
Recession	**2001M06–2002M07**	**-1.437%**	**0.013877**
Growth	2002M08–2004M12	0.471%	0.296711
Recession	**2005M01–2005M11**	**-0.362%**	**0.134181**
Growth	2005M12–2006M12	0.267%	0.100952
Recession	**2007M01–2009M09**	**-0.188%**	**0.358052**
Growth	2009M10–2014M01	0.138%	0.507764

economy and market also performed better due to improved oil prices. However, with the increase in liquidity, the Jordanian market experienced a substantial increase in price volatility in 2005, which lead to a bubble. This increase in price volatility also increased the level of market integration, following which the bubble burst and the level of integration dropped in line with the economic recession of that period. This was exacerbated further by increasing oil prices coupled with a reduction in external grants.

In the 2007 and 2008 crisis period, the drop in market integration is attributable again to significant drops in oil prices. Post-crisis, the level of integration did rise once again, but not as strongly as the other countries. Overall, the Jordanian stock market is not highly integrated with the world index.

Other OIC Member Countries

In the earlier period of this study, for the countries in Table 6.10, the integration is more than one, indicating zero integration owing to a low number of companies listed on the stock exchange. The remaining OIC member countries depict weak levels of integrations with high short-term fluctuations owing to the emerging nature of their markets. Their markets are exposed considerably to volatile inflows.

Like the other countries in the sample, a commonality amongst these OIC countries is that the integration levels shot up in 2008–2010 resultant of the contagion effect from the global transmission of shocks of the crisis. The rationale behind this persistent high-integration can be due to the regime uncertainty during the Euro crisis.

Developed Countries

Pressing forward, in Table 6.11, the three developed nations selected showed high levels of integration throughout the study period with only the UK showing a significant dip in market integration levels in 2006 relatable to the peak oil crisis of 2006. Oil prices increased drastically caused mainly by speculation by hedge-fund managers. A similar episode is seen in 1999–2000 period whereby the 1987 stock market crash in the USA almost caused a global financial crisis.

Another observation on the developed countries is the smoother variation of integration process over time. This suggests substantially less investment restrictions for these countries. Furthermore, during the crisis period of 2008 onwards, all three developed countries showed the same

Table 6.10 Business cycles and integration: Kuwait, Oman and Saudi Arabia

Kuwait		*Average growth*	*Integration*
Growth	1999M01–1999M10	1.049%	-N/A-
Recession	**1999M11–2001M04**	**−1.032%**	**-N/A-**
Growth	2001M05–2005M02	0.286%	0.3516
Recession	**2005M03–2006M04**	**−0.556%**	**0.2013**
Growth	2006M05–2007M05	0.673%	0.0680
Recession	**2007M06–2009M04**	**−0.501%**	**0.1456**
Growth	2009M05–2010M12	0.610%	0.6296
Recession	**2011M01–2014M12**	**−0.187%**	0.4906
Oman		*Average growth*	*Integration*
Recession	**1999M01–1999M08**	−0.175%	-N/A-
Growth	1999M09–2000M09	0.624%	-N/A-
Recession	**2000M10–2001M08**	−0.501%	-N/A-
Growth	2001M09–2002M05	0.243%	-N/A-
Recession	**2002M06–2004M05**	−0.276%	0.2348
Growth	2004M06–2005M08	0.673%	0.3471
Recession	**2005M09–2007M06**	−0.385%	0.2045
Growth	2007M08–2010M01	0.201%	0.4192
Recession	**2010M02–2011M12**	−0.219%	0.6611
Growth	2012M01–2014M12	0.287%	0.8281
Saudi Arabia		*Average growth*	*Integration*
Growth	1999M01-1999M10	1.049%	-N/A-
Recession	**1999M11 2001M04**	**-1.032%**	**-N/A-**
Growth	2001M05-2005M02	0.286%	0.3516
Recession	**2005M03 2006M04**	**-0.556%**	**0.2013**
Growth	2006M05-2007M05	0.673%	0.0680
Recession	**2007M06 2009M04**	**-0.501%**	**0.1456**
Growth	2009M05-2012M3	0.553%	0.7199
Recession	**2012M04-2014M12**	**-0.802%**	0.3829

degree of integration. The financial crisis had uniformly increased comovements between already highly cointegrated stock markets.

6.8.2 *Regional Integration*

The above analysis describes how the OIC member countries are integrated with the world average. However, the results are insufficient as most of the countries in the sample maybe more integrated regionally than with the

Table 6.11 Business cycles and integration: the UK, France and Germany

UK		*Average growth*	*Integration*
Growth	1999M01–1999M12	0.380%	0.7881
Recession	**2000M01–2003M03**	**-0.015%**	**0.8355**
Growth	2003M04–2004M06	0.154%	0.9063
Recession	**2004M07–2005M03**	**-0.111%**	**0.8656**
Growth	2005M04–2007M12	0.187%	0.6767
Recession	**2008M01–2009M06**	**-0.633%**	**0.8679**
Growth	2009M07–2010M10	0.508%	0.9660
Recession	2011M01–2014M12	**-0.060%**	**0.8982**
France		*Average growth*	*Integration*
Growth	1999M01–2000M11	0.189%	0.7928
Recession	**2000M12–2003M09**	-0.173%	0.8805
Growth	2003M10–2008M03	0.192%	0.8973
Recession	**2008M04–2009M07**	-1.092%	0.9419
Growth	2009M08–2014M12	0.299%	0.9412
Germany		*Average growth*	*Integration*
Growth	1999M01–200012	0.413%	0.7393
Recession	**2001M01–2003M09**	**-0.324%**	**0.8729**
Growth	2003M10–2008M03	0.287%	0.8399
Recession	**2008M04–2009M08**	**-1.556%**	**0.9022**
Growth	2009M09–2011M08	0.785%	0.9252
Recession	**2011M09–2014M12**	**-0.771%**	**0.8808**

world average. Hence, to account for this, the correlation of each sample country with United States, Asia-Pacific and European Union (EU) are used to understand the level of integration OIC member countries have with these regions. In the tables below, the integration with each region is presented in conjunction with the business cycle phase of each country. Owing to a substantial lack of data, Bangladesh had to be removed from the current analysis on regional integration.

Malaysia

Table 6.12 details the level of integration between Malaysia and the USA, Asia-Pacific region and the European Union (EU). Interestingly, low level of integration throughout the sample period is seen, in particular for the region of USA and EU.

Table 6.12 Business cycle and regional integration: Malaysia

		Integration		
		USA	*Asia-Pacific*	*EU*
Growth	1999M01–2000M08	0.002	0.273	0.122
Recession	**2000M9–2002M1**	**0.014**	**0.195**	**0.016**
Growth	2002M02–2004M06	0.000	0.360	0.160
Recession	**2004 M7–2005M6**	**0.030**	**0.341**	**0.242**
Growth	2005M07–2006M06	0.000	0.256	0.093
Recession	**2006 M7–2007M3**	**0.043**	**0.476**	**0.278**
Growth	2007M04–2008M03	0.063	0.643	0.393
Recession	**2008M4–2009M5**	**0.119**	**0.546**	**0.398**
Growth	2009M06–2010M06	0.225	0.514	0.333
Recession	**2010M07–2011M03**	**0.179**	**0.475**	**0.261**
Growth	2011M04–2012M12	0.082	0.490	0.191

Integration with the US market remained low in the first half of the sample period, but stronger integration is seen after the financial crisis of 2008. The significantly low integration in 1999 with the USA can be explained by the capital controls placed in Malaysia after the 1997 crisis, which caused foreign influence to be at a minimum. The degree of integration between Malaysia and the USA is higher during financial recessions than financial booms.

This is indicated during the growth period of 2009–2010, which was still affected by the crisis and Malaysia had the highest integration with the USA at this phase. Similar results are seen for the EU, whereby Malaysia is highly integrated with EU markets in the recession of 2008–2009 brought on by the global economic crisis.

Much higher levels of integration are seen between Malaysia and Asia-Pacific region, owing mainly to high levels of intraregional trade amongst the ASEAN countries, higher peaks of integration are seen after the global crisis. It is during the 2007–2008 growth phase that has the highest level of integration of Malaysia with the Asia-Pacific region at 0.64. It was reported by the Pacific Economic Cooperation Council that Malaysia was the sixth most integrated economy within the Asia-Pacific region.

Indonesia

Indonesia shows similar results to that of Malaysia, whereby integration is higher for Asia-Pacific region than the other two and that integration levels rose post-crisis period. From Table 6.13, it is understood that the market was

Table 6.13 Business cycle and regional integration: Indonesia

		Integration		
		USA	*Asia-Pacific*	*EU*
Growth	1999M01–2000M10	0.000	0.188	0.076
Recession	**2000M11–2003M04**	0.012	0.210	0.068
Growth	2003M05–2006M07	0.081	0.370	0.229
Recession	**2006M08–2007M08**	0.068	0.585	0.363
Growth	2007M09–2008M08	0.111	0.540	0.371
Recession	**2008M09–2009M08**	0.195	0.581	0.398
Growth	2009M09–2010M07	0.161	0.590	0.341
Recession	**2010M08–2014M12**	0.203	0.584	0.328

highly integrated with the USA in the recession phase of 2010–2012 post-crisis. Similarly, an integration level of 0.398 was seen with Indonesia during the recession of 2008–2009 with EU markets and with Asia-Pacific at 0.59 in 2009–2010.

The lowest level of integration with the US market is seen during the 2000 recession period, following a series of unfortunate events that shattered investor confidence; World Trade Centre terrorist attacks, dotcom crisis, collapse of Enron and perhaps more importantly the Bali bombings. All of which severely reduced the integration level.

The following period sees a significant increase in integration with all three regions, explicable through Indonesia's opening economy, allowing more foreign trade. However, this too did not last long as in 2006; the Indonesian economy took a hit from the effects of the tsunami, and its own internal crisis.

Pakistan

The integration between Pakistan and the USA and EU are highest during the recession of 2005–2008, owing mainly to crisis of 2008. Furthermore, it was during this period that Pakistan received its highest foreign direct investments, culminating to US$8.4 billion in 2006 and 2007. An increasing level of integration is seen with the Asia-Pacific region, with significant increases post-global crisis, the highest being in the growth phase of 2011–2012 at 0.246.

As show in Table 6.14, the overall integration of Pakistan with developed markets remains low throughout the sample period as the Pakistani market is still developing and has met with several turbulences. Particularly,

Table 6.14 Business cycle and regional integration: Pakistan

		Integration		
		USA	*Asia-Pacific*	*EU*
Growth	1999M06–2000M05	0.000	0.017	0.038
Recession	**2000M06–2002M12**	0.000	0.012	0.045
Growth	2003M01–2005M06	0.031	0.092	0.080
Recession	**2005M07–2008M03**	0.057	0.102	0.092
Growth	2008M04–2010M05	0.050	0.143	0.034
Recession	**2010M06–2011M04**	0.024	0.045	0.045
Growth	2011M05–2012M03	0.023	0.246	0.082
Recession	**2012M04–2014M12**	0.000	0.151	0.000

in the recession phase of 2000–2002 where the integration with the USA was zero, this is understood by the withdrawal of US investors after the September 11 attacks, and the dotcom crisis. Similarly, Pakistan appears not to be significantly integrated with European markets.

Turkey

Owing to the more developed nature of Turkey's stock market and economy than the other three countries discussed above, its integration with the USA shows larger values. After the global crisis, in the 2008–2009, the Turkish market is highly integrated with the USA at 0.41 Similarly, Turkey reflects higher levels of integration post-crisis for all three regions. It is in the recessionary phase of 2010 that Turkey has its highest levels of integration with Asia-Pacific and EU.

Table 6.15 Business cycle and regional integration: Turkey

		Integration		
		USA	*Asia-Pacific*	*EU*
Growth	1999M01–1999M07	0.000	0.082	0.147
Recession	**1999M08–2000M08**	0.046	0.144	0.185
Growth	2000M09–2003M03	0.000	0.162	0.120
Recession	**2003M04–2004M03**	0.118	0.140	0.204
Growth	2004M04–2006M12	0.370	0.221	0.457
Recession	**2007M01–2008M04**	0.340	0.191	0.540
Growth	2008M05–2010M09	0.406	0.322	0.594
Recession	**2010M10–2014M12**	0.336	0.406	0.619

Table 6.15 shows that the Turkish market is more integrated with the EU than the other two regions, owing first to geographical regions, and second, EU's interest in Turkey. Since Turkey's accession negotiation in 2005, integration with the EU has been increasing.

After 2005, the foreign direct investment to Turkey had reached US$ 52.2 billion which had a positive effect on the Turkish economy and this is reflected in the high levels of integration throughout the three regions, with the highest being with EU at 0.457. Interestingly, it is also at this time, that its integration with US market increased with a jump in integration from 0.118 to 0.37.

Jordan

From Table 6.16, the Jordanian market remains severely disintegrated from the major regions of the world. This is attributable to higher domestic trade and regional trade (i.e. within its geographical boundaries). The increasing oil prices in 2003 and 2004 explain the increased integration in the growth phase of 2002–2004, which is significant increase from the previous periods having no integration at all.

Furthermore, after the September 11 attacks, several Arab nations were reluctant to invest in US markets and vice versa, hence most Arab nations invested in their neighbouring markets. With the massive influx of investments in 2005, the Jordanian market collapsed resulting in no integration with any of the three regions. Similarly, in the throngs of the global financial crisis, the integration with US market became zero, only to rise post-crisis to 0.012.

Table 6.16 Business cycle and regional integration: Jordan

		Integration		
		USA	*Asia-Pacific*	*EU*
Growth	1999M02–2001M05	0.000	0.000	0.000
Recession	**2001M06–2002M07**	0.000	0.000	0.000
Growth	2002M08–2004M12	0.087	0.092	0.082
Recession	**2005M01–2005M11**	0.000	0.000	0.000
Growth	2005M12–2006M12	0.058	0.012	0.000
Recession	**2007M01–2009M09**	0.000	0.164	0.085
Growth	2009M10–2014M01	0.012	0.116	0.043

Egypt

Interestingly, the Egyptian market is highly integrated with all three regions in the post-crisis growth phase of 2009–2010, at 0.25 for the USA, 0.39 for Asia-Pacific and 0.37 for EU. This is in line with theory whereby markets become more integrated post-crisis. However, integration falls in the following period, owing mainly to the political and economic instability in Egypt and the start of the Arab Spring. Furthermore, several of Egypt's giant corporations were listed in foreign markets, such as in London and New York, which explains the larger value of integration during the crisis period.

Similarly, in Table 6.17, a plunge in integration is seen with the three regions from the growth phase in 2000 to the recession phase in 2002–2004, falling several points below. This dramatic drop can be explained by the hesitance of foreign investors to invest in Egypt following the September 11 attacks, the sluggish nature of privatization and political circumstances in the Middle East region during that time.

Kuwait

Due to a lack in data, as seen in Table 6.18, the results for Kuwait is circumscribed from 2005–2012, providing a shorter time span to analyse. The period of 2005–2007 shows declining integration with all three regions, owing to the Jordanian stock market crash of 2005. This had a strong impact on the Kuwaiti market as well, and it shook investor confidence. However, this indicates integration between the two markets. The lower levels of integration with the USA, Asia-Pacific and EU can be explained by the strong position of domestic investors in Kuwait. Furthermore, there are major barriers to foreign investments, which limited

Table 6.17 Business cycle and regional integration: Egypt

		Integration		
		USA	*Asia-Pacific*	*EU*
Recession	**1999M01–2000M03**	0.033	0.097	0.123
Growth	2000M04–2001M12	0.032	0.107	0.083
Recession	**2002M01–2004M02**	0.014	0.081	0.006
Growth	2004M03–2008M02	0.013	0.160	0.091
Recession	**2008M03–2009M04**	0.123	0.357	0.274
Growth	2009M05–2010M08	0.249	0.387	0.365
Recession	**2010M09–2014M04**	0.127	0.213	0.172

Table 6.18 Business cycle and regional integration: Kuwait

		Integration		
		USA	*Asia-Pacific*	*EU*
Recession	**2005M03–2006M04**	0.008	0.041	0.080
Growth	2006M05–2007M05	0.000	0.000	0.016
Recession	**2007M06–2009M04**	0.073	0.008	0.126
Growth	2009M05–2010M12	0.108	0.042	0.099
Recession	**2011M01–2012M12**	0.073	0.039	0.056

the integration to a certain extent. This is reflected in the integration of the markets post crisis, while the integration went up, it did so to a lesser extent than other countries with more open markets.

Saudi Arabia

Like Kuwait, Saudi Arabia shows significantly lower levels of integration with the three regions on average, in Table 6.19. Saudi Arabia's market is closed off for foreign investors, thus limiting the integration with major regions of the world. With a strong domestic base, the Tawadul has been a noteworthy player in the OIC.

The absence of integration during the growth phase of 2006–2007 is attributable to the collapse of the market in 2006, in an event known as Riyadh's Black Monday. With massive amounts of oil money, domestic investors put all their money in the stock market causing a bubble, which eventually burst owing partly to the unsophisticated nature of the market, and the market collapsed.

Table 6.19 Business cycle and regional integration: Saudi Arabia

		Integration		
		USA	*Asia-Pacific*	*EU*
Growth	1999M01–1999M10	0.031	0.028	0.007
Recession	**1999M11–2001M04**	0.000	0.095	0.107
Growth	2001M05–2005M02	0.036	0.057	0.039
Recession	**2005M03–2006M04**	0.039	0.017	0.021
Growth	2006M05–2007M05	0.000	0.000	0.000
Recession	**2007M06–2009M04**	0.073	0.132	0.090
Growth	2009M05–2012M3	0.182	0.250	0.255
Recession	**2012M04–2014M12**	0.076	0.188	0.169

While, the Saudi market was not affected greatly with the global crisis, you can still see a spike in integration with all three regions during the post-crisis period of 2009–2012. Similarly, higher integration is seen during the 2001–2005 growth phase, caused mainly by the dotcom crisis, spike in oil prices and the September 11 attacks.

Oman

In line with the literature, the integration with the USA, Asia-Pacific and EU regions reaches a peak during the post-crisis recession of 2010–2011, as seen in Table 6.20. Interestingly, there is a significant decline in integration during the 2001–2005 period owing the several reasons. First, this period entails the September 11 attacks, second, fluctuating oil prices and, third, there are few firms listed on the Omani stock exchange to validate a significant integration.

Developed Countries

Table 6.21 shows that the market of developed country is significantly more integrated with other more developed markets or regions. All three sample countries are highly integrated with the USA and EU markets. In particular, as these countries are a part of the EU, the level of integration is almost equal to one, which is the highest level of integration. The integration of these markets with the USA also yields high levels of integration

Table 6.20 Business cycle and regional integration: Oman

		Integration		
		USA	*Asia-Pacific*	*EU*
Recession	**1999M01–1999M08**	0.028	0.000	0.000
Growth	1999M09–2000M09	0.015	0.000	0.000
Recession	**2000M10–2001M08**	0.011	0.075	0.113
Growth	2001M09–2002M05	0.000	0.041	0.000
Recession	**2002M06–2004M05**	0.000	0.010	0.000
Growth	2004M06–2005M08	0.000	0.076	0.000
Recession	**2005M09–2007M06**	0.110	0.000	0.056
Growth	2007M08–2010M01	0.036	0.212	0.107
Recession	**2010M02–2011M12**	0.134	0.276	0.165
Growth	2012M01–2014M12	0.091	0.197	0.079

Table 6.21 Business cycle and regional integration: UK, France, Germany

UK		*Integration*		
		USA	*Asia-Pacific*	*EU*
Recession	**1999M01–1999M12**	0.360	0.230	0.756
Growth	2000M01–2003M03	0.447	0.233	0.829
Recession	**2003M04–2004M05**	0.421	0.280	0.726
Growth	2004M06–2005M04	0.337	0.257	0.641
Recession	**2005M05–2007M12**	0.481	0.317	0.779
Growth	2008M01–2009M07	0.531	0.349	0.892
Recession	**2009M08–2010M10**	0.681	0.353	0.906
Growth	2010M11–2014M12	0.687	0.418	0.873

France		*Integration*		
		USA	*Asia-Pacific*	*EU*
Growth	1999M01–2000M11	0.391	0.221	0.736
Recession	**2000M12–2003M09**	0.520	0.179	0.840
Growth	2003M10–2008M03	0.456	0.283	0.731
Recession	**2008M04–2009M07**	0.598	0.330	0.894
Growth	2009M08–2014M12	0.708	0.357	0.906

Germany		*Integration*		
		USA	*Asia-Pacific*	*EU*
Growth	1999M01–2000M12	0.19	0.22	0.44
Recession	**2001M01–2003M09**	0.42	0.22	0.61
Growth	2003M10–2008M03	0.37	0.39	0.67
Recession	**2008M04–2009M08**	0.55	0.38	0.84
Growth	2009M09–2011M08	0.64	0.43	0.83
Recession	**2011M09–2014M12**	0.67	0.45	0.88

with a significant increase in the post crisis period of 2009–2010. Similarly, its integration with the EU also reaches its highest in the same period.

An integration of 0.44 is observed for Germany in its growth phase of 1999–2000 as this was the period, when the two-divided Germany's reunited, following which, German markets remained highly integrated throughout the rest of the sample period. The sample developed countries and its integration with Asia-Pacific region remain lower than the other two regions owing to low investment in Asia-Pacific.

6.9 Conclusion

The chapter aims to measure the degree of integration for both Islamic and developed countries within ICAMP captured by the rolling R^2. Analysing the market integrations through the various significant economic breaks provided insight on which countries are more integrated, thus allowing policymakers and investors to move towards those countries at the opportune times.

The results show that within the OIC, only Malaysia, Indonesia and Turkey showed high levels of integration with relatively small variations over time. Meanwhile, the other OIC member countries seemed confined to low levels of market integration showing a lack of financial openness, restrictions to foreign investments. Furthermore, it is observed most of the Arab member countries followed similar patterns of stock market volatility and integration indicating a cointegrating relationship between them. This acts as an impediment to economic growth of such countries. Emerging countries are volatile by nature and to allow for further growth and smoother fluctuations, financial liberalization is called for.

Another observation from this study is most of the markets became more integrated during the crisis period of 2008. This is supported by past research that claims international markets become more correlated during economic downturns (see Longin and Solnik, 2001)

Notes

1. See Kleimeier and Sander (2000) and Centeno and Mello (1999)
2. See Imbs (2004), Kose et al. (2003)
3. See Ferson and Harvey (1991, 1993)
4. See De Santis and Gerard (1997), Engel and Rodrigues (1989)
5. See Guesmi and Teulon (2014), and Rizvi, et al. (2014).

References

Adler, M., & Dumas, B. (1983). International portfolio choice and corporation finance: A synthesis. *Journal of Finance, 38*(3), 925–984.

Avakian, A., Podobnik, B., Piskor, M., & Stanley, H. E.. (2014). Capital death in the world market. *Physics Review E, 89*, 032805.

Bodnar, G., Dumas, B., & Marston, R. (2003). Cross-border valuation: The international cost of equity capital (Working Paper No. 10115). Resource

Document. National Bureau of Economic Research. http://www.nber.org/papers/w10115.pdf. Accessed 25 June 2016.

Bollerslev, T., Engle, R. F., & Wooldridge, J. M. (1988). A capital asset pricing model with time-varying covariances. *Journal of Political Economy, 96*, 116–131.

Bruner, R. F., Wei, L., Kirtzman, M., Myrgren, S., & Page, S. (2008). Market integration in developed and emerging markets: Evidence from the CAPM. *Emerging Markets Review, 9*(2), 89–103.

Centeno, M., & Mello, A. (1999). How integrated are the money market and the bank loans within the European Union? *Journal of International Money and Finance, 18*(1), 45–106.

De Santis, G., & Gerard, B. (1997). How big is the premium for currency risk? *Journal of Financial Economics, 49*, 375–412.

Engel, C., & Rodrigues, A. (1989). Tests of international CAPM with time-varying covariances. *Journal of Applied Econometrics, 4*(2), 119–138.

Fama, E. F., & French, K. R. (2004). The capital asset pricing model: theory and evidence. *The Journal of Economic Perspectives, 18*(3), 25–46.

Ferson, W. E., & Harvey, C. R. (1991). The variation of economic risk premiums. *Journal of Political Economy, 99*(2), 385–415.

Ferson, W. E., & Harvey, C. R. (1993). The risk and predictability of international equity returns. *Review of Financial Studies, 6*, 527–566.

Frijins, B., Tourani-Rad, A., & Indriawan, I. (2012). Political crises and the stock market integration of emerging markets. *Journal of Banking and Finance, 36*(3), 644–653.

Gentzoglanis, A. (2007). Financial integration, regulation and competitiveness in Middle East and North Africa countries. *Managerial Finance, 33*(7), 461–476.

Gokcen, S., & Ozturkmen, A. (1997). Integration versus segmentation: Istanbul stock exchange. *Borsa Istanbul Review, 1*(1), 97–106.

Guesmi, K., & Teulon, F. (2014). *The determinants of regional stock market integration in middle east: A conditional ICAPM approach*. IPAG Working Paper No. 214. IPAG Business School.

Hassan, A., & Javed, M. T. (2010). Relationships among equity markets of emerging OIC economies. *Pakistan Journal of Applied Economics, 20*(1&2), 29–46.

Imbs, J. (2004). *The Real Effects of Financial Integration*. CEPR Papers 4335. C.E.P.R. Discussion Papers.

Kleimeier, S., & Sander, H. (2000). Regionalisation versus globalisation in European financial market integration: Evidence from co-integration analyses. *Journal of Banking and Finance, 24*(6), 1005–1043.

Koedijk, K., Kool, C., Schotman, P., & Van Dijk, M. (2002). The cost of capital in international financial markets: Local or global?. *Journal of International Money and Finance, 21*(6), 905–929.

Kose, A. M., Prasad, E. S., & Terrones, M. E. (2003). *How Does Globalization Affect the Synchronization of Business Cycles?* IMF Working Paper No. 27. International Monetary Fund.

Lintner, J. (1965). The valuation of risk assets and the selection of risky investments in stock portfolios and capital budgets. *Review of Economics and Statistics, 47*(1), 13–37.

Longin, F., & Solnik, B. (1995). Is the correlation in international equity returns constant: 1970–1990?. *Journal of International Money and Finance, 14*(1), 3–26.

Neaime, S. (2002). Liberalization and financial integration of MENA stock markets. In *Regional trade, finance and labor markets.* Proceedings of the Economic Research Forum (ERF) Ninth Annual Conference, Al Sharjah, UAE, October, 26–28.

Pukthuanthong, K., & Roll, R. (2009). Global market integration: an alternative measure and its application. *Journal of Financial Economics, 94*(2), 214–232.

Rizvi, S. A. R., Dewandaru, G., Bacha, O. I., & Masih, M. (2014). An analysis of stock market efficiency: Developed vs islamic stock markets using MF-DFA. *Physica A, 407*, 86–99.

Robson, P. (1980). *The economics of international integration.* London: Allen and Unwin.

Sharpe, W. F. (1964). Capital asset Prices: A theory of market equilibrium under conditions of risk. *Journal of Finance, 19*(3), 425–442.

Solnik, B. H. (1974). An equilibrium model of the international capital model. *Journal of Economic Theory, 8*(4), 500–524.

Stulz, R. M. (1981). A model of international asset pricing. *Journal of Financial Economics, 9*, 383–406.

CHAPTER 7

Conclusion

Abstract In an endeavour to have an enriched understanding of the stock markets of Organization of Islamic Cooperation (OIC) countries, this book looks into the relationship between stock markets and business cycles of OIC member countries across three platforms, namely, volatility, efficiency and integration. The results show us that in all three measures, the stock markets are improving over the years. However, there is room for improvement. OIC member countries can benefit from more liberalized and cleaner markets, improved regulations and increased intra-regional trade.

Keywords Stock market development · Liberalization · Clean market · Increased liquidity

The objective of this book is to examine the relationship between business cycle and stock market performance of Islamic countries. The countries selected are from Organization of Islamic Cooperation (OIC) regional bloc. The OIC has the potential to outperform other regional blocs, with several members characterized as rapidly emerging markets. However, the OIC does not have the proper foundations to allow for such rapid development. The underdevelopment and inefficiency of its stock market holds OIC from performing proficiently, as an inefficient stock market does not allow for optimal resource allocation.

S. Arshad, *Stock Markets in Islamic Countries*, Palgrave CIBFR Studies in Islamic Finance, DOI 10.1007/978-3-319-47803-6_7

In an attempt to achieve the objective, which aims to analyse the relationship between business cycles and stock markets, the analysis is conducted across three imperative platforms; volatility, efficiency and integration. These three platforms are inter-related as high volatility can cause inefficiency in the stock market, and an inefficient stock market does not allow for optimal resource allocation and thus inhibiting economic growth. Furthermore, owing to globalization, increases in volatility in one market can cause increases in markets worldwide, giving significance to market integration of stock markets. Hence, understanding the relations of efficiency, integration and volatility of a market with the different phases of the economy will allow investors to make more informed investment decisions.

The analysis shows us that in terms of volatility, most of the countries saw its business cycle and stock markets fluctuating owing to drops and increases in world oil prices. Furthermore, all the countries in the sample are affected by the global crisis, some to a lesser extent than others. In regard to efficiency, the analysis reveals overall the countries show a trend of improving efficiency throughout the sample period. Furthermore, countries with more developed markets, such as Malaysia and Indonesia, fared better than their counterparts even during the Asian financial crisis. Similarly, oil-producing countries were often less efficient when oil prices were volatile.

Lastly, this book aimed to measure the degree of integration for both Islamic and developed countries using International Capital Asset Pricing Model (ICAMP) captured by the rolling R^2. The results showed that within the OIC, only Malaysia, Indonesia and Turkey showed high levels of integration with relatively small variations over time. Meanwhile, the other OIC member countries seemed confined to low levels of market integration showing a lack of financial openness, restrictions to foreign investments. Furthermore, it is observed that most of the Arab member countries followed similar patterns of stock market volatility and integration indicating a cointegrating relationship between them. This acts as an impediment to economic growth of such countries.

The outcomes of this study raise a number of policy issues and recommendations to fortify the relationship between stock markets and business cycles and its implication for the OIC. The macroeconomic nature of stock markets call for a more enabling atmosphere to fully realize its potential. Many countries in the OIC currently either do not have stock markets or have stock markets with little volume and or are closed to foreign investment. Stock markets should be deregulated allowing the market forces of demand and supply to function without interferences. Liberalization of the stock markets will increase the inflow of foreign capital leading to healthier stock market development and in turn greater economic growth.

The barriers to entry for new exchanges should be eliminated to nurture a more competitive atmosphere in the market. This may affect the best execution rules of trading decisions so that different trading platforms are chosen to best meet the investors' needs. Gradually with the aid of increased competition, trading cost would also reduce.

Furthermore, it is essential to ensure market cleanliness by enhancing supervision to achieve transparency, which will allow for higher market integration. At the same time, the legislation quality should also be improved, for instance, the time it takes the court to enforce a contract. This would provide investors with protection and consequently increase the market confidence.

Another opportunity to develop their stock markets would be to bring about financial openness. Keeping in mind, that most of the OIC member countries are emerging markets with recently founded financial markets, opening the markets to foreign participation could be beneficial.

While many argue that financial openness might be harmful for countries with mediocre development in financial markets as seen in the recent debt and financial crises, it would be beneficial for OIC member countries to open up their markets, as it would allow them to draw in substantial foreign direct investments (FDIs). With the shift in investment from developed to developing countries, the OIC member countries are a viable financial investment.

However, financial openness is only one side of the coin, while it may increase stock market activity, which would in turn benefit the economy, the OIC would also benefit from a more open trading cycle, in particular with other member countries. Currently, the level of trade amongst member countries is low, with many preferring to trade to non-member countries. The abject development and economic performance of most of the 57 member countries since its commencement can be attributed to, inter alia, incompatible economic policies of the countries.

Moreover, despite the lure of financial openness, there are certain issues that need to be taken into consideration first. It is known that it was the procyclical capital flows that were responsible for the shock transmission in the propagation during the crisis, in particular for emerging countries.

Choosing to focus on short-term gains could jeopardize the needs for long-term growth. This could explain the volatile pattern of integration over time for Islamic countries. Volatile inflows may lead to volatile consumption, investment and eventually growth of the country, inadvertently resulting in welfare losses and high social cost.

This derives its rationality from the violation of idealistic assumptions on perfect markets and perfect inter-temporal smoothing, since markets are often always exposed to cadenced rise and fall, externalities and coordination failures. The situation is worsened for OIC member countries that do not have a prudent institutional facility and have complete risk markets to mitigate. The market would therefore, not be self-regulating and judicious countercyclical policies should be implemented.

From a policy aspect, an efficient market is essential since, it can play an important role in the development of the economy, via resource allocation and capital formation, and distribution of wealth channels. The stock markets play a pivotal role in increasing savings and investment, which are essential for economic development. From an international investor perspective, the equity market, by allowing diversification across a variety of assets, helps reduce the risk the investors must bear, thus reducing the cost of capital, which in turn spurs investment and economic growth. There is the need to ensure strong and adequate supervision by the regulatory authorities. This would prevent any stock price bubble while as the same time it would ensure that information about stock price is a true reflection of the value of shares. In addition, there is the need for a greater development of the OIC common stock market through appropriate policies, which would enhance the efficiency of the market.

The results imply that an economic boom influences the resource allocation positively with an improvement in the efficiency and a lesser volatile nature of the stock markets. An interesting finding of this study argues on the impact of volatility on long term on inefficiency of the long-term component of the stock market. The long-term component of the investor profile, are generally assumed to be the investors which enter the OIC markets on the basis of the fundamental economic growth and not with a short-term return orientation. From a sustainable economic growth perspective the policymakers need to address the concerns of the investors focused on long term, and move towards structural changes which governs their investment behaviour.

Governance has been categorized as a critical determinant of attracting investment into the real sector on long-term sustainability level, and a steady positive development on this aspect may lead to a reposed confidence of long-term investors, which would result in reduced volatility thus improving the efficiency of the markets in the region.

The OIC has become disadvantageous with small volume of intra-bloc trade and unable to achieve economies of scales on its own. The increase in inter-market trade would prove a unique solution for the member countries to attain substantial gains from international trade. The OIC has the potential of becoming the largest diversified economic bloc in recent times. Member countries would benefit from strengthening their Islamic ties to achieve socio-economic solidarity, allowing self-sufficiency and reducing economic dependence on non-Islamic countries for import and export.

The present study has its limitations; first, this study only encompasses a small fraction of 57 member countries, which does not provide a complete picture of all the OIC member countries. Second, due to the lack of availability of data, several years were lost in this study limiting the reach of the analysis to a maximum of 22 years only.

Future research can benefit from having more than one indicator of economic activity and a more rigorous bandpass filter to provide a more accurate understanding of the vicissitudes in a business cycle. In addition, researchers can benefit from addressing the calendar effect and incorporating the contagion effect in the analysis. The contagion effect is mentioned briefly but requires a more in-depth analysis. While all the countries in this analysis was selected based on their market capitalization share, further research can benefit from including several more OIC member states in their analysis.

Index

S. Arshad, *Stock Markets in Islamic Countries,* Palgrave CIBFR Studies in Islamic Finance, DOI 10.1007/978-3-319-47803-6